lemon *zest* 6

lemon *zest*

More than 175 recipes with a *twist*

lori longbotham

broadway books
new york

BROADWAY

Broadway Books titles may be purchased for business or promotional use or for special sales. For information, please write to: Special Markets Department, Random
House, Inc., 1540 Broadway, New York, NY 10036.

PRINTED IN THE UNITED STATES OF AMERICA

"A Lemon" from SELECTED POEMS of Pablo Neruda, translated by Ben Belitt.
Copyright © 1961 by Ben Belitt. Used by permission of Grove Atlantic, Inc.

BROADWAY BOOKS and its logo, a letter B bisected on the diagonal, are trademarks of
Broadway Books, a division of Random House, Inc.

Visit our website at www.broadwaybooks.com

Library of Congress Cataloging-in-Publication Data
Longbotham, Lori
Lemon zest : more than 175 recipes with a twist / Lori Longbotham.—1st ed.
p. cm.
1. Cookery (Lemons)   I. Title.
TX813.L4 L66 2001
641.6'4334—dc21   00-069763

FIRST EDITION

Book design and art by JUDITH STAGNITTO ABBATE / ABBATE DESIGN

ISBN 0-7679-0617-9

1   3   5   7   9   10   8   6   4   2

For Jerry—my
favorite traveling companion,
no matter what the journey

a lemon | PABLO NERUDA

Out of lemon flowers
loosed
on the moonlight, love's
lashed and insatiable
essences,
sodden with fragrance,
the lemon tree's yellow
emerges,
the lemons
move down
from the tree's planetarium.

Delicate merchandise!
The harbors are big with it—
bazaars
for the light and the
barbarous gold.
We open
the halves
of a miracle,
and a clotting of acids
brims
into the starry
divisions:
creation's
original juices
irreducible, changeless,
alive:

so the freshness lives on
in a lemon,
in the sweet-smelling house of the rind,
the proportions, arcane and acerb.

Cutting the lemon
the knife
leaves a little
cathedral:
alcoves unguessed by the eye
that open acidulous glass
to the light; topazes
riding the droplets,
altars,
aromatic facades.
So, while the hand
holds the cut of the lemon,
half a world
on a trencher,
the gold of the universe
wells
to your touch:
a cup yellow
with miracles,
a breast and a nipple
perfuming the earth;
a flashing made fruitage,
the diminutive fire of a planet.

Contents

Acknowledgments

First thanks to Angela Miller, Jennifer Josephy, Joan Ward, and Anne Resnik for tremendous help and inspiration.

Thanks to my zesty friends Deborah Mintcheff, Judith Sutton, Barbara Ottenhoff, Barbara Howe, Marie Regusis, Sarah Mahoney, Jean Galton, Pat Dailey, Sabra Turnbull, Valerie Cippolone, Carol Kramer, Lisa Troland, Susan Westmoreland, John Avery, Rosey, Sprocket, and Tracy Seaman—all have the pefect balance of sweet and tart and a wonderful twist.

With gratitude to Auntie Jean, Steve and Liz, Mom and Ken, and Dad.

Handy in size, available all year round,
inexpensive, long-lasting,
and perfectly packaged in a tough skin
which is as valuable as the juice it contains,
a lemon is the ideal household implement,
an honorable standard against which
all patented inventions
might be measured.

—MARGARET VISSER
Much Depends on Dinner

lemon zest

Introduction

everything about a lemon is lovely: its shape, its flavor, its color, and its fragrance. A lemon is a culinary treasure. How tasteless and boring life would be without lemons. Not only do they enhance and reveal other flavors by balancing sweetness and richness, but their aroma, intense flavor, and piquancy add a freshness that is absolutely necessary to good food. The lemon is, unquestionably, the most versatile of all the fruits of the earth. It's really two fruits in one: you get both the aromatic flavor of the zest and the spirited zing of the juice. With the wide range of exotic produce now available from all over the world, the humble lemon is taken for granted, yet its full flavor, acidic juice, and zesty rind set it apart as an indispensable fruit for any cook.

Lemons evoke sun-kissed climates and seem to bring with them the very character of the places they grow. The sparklers of the fruit world, they remind me of all things cool and fresh.

Often I walk into the market and grab a couple of lemons, then figure out what to cook. With my lemons in hand, I can head to the seafood counter or the meat case, to the produce aisle or the dairy section. I rarely find myself making a full meal without using a lemon, and I have no problem with using lemons in more than one dish for the same meal.

Adding lemon to someone else's cooking almost always improves it. Say you're picking up a roast chicken from a take-out shop. Serve it with a wedge or two of lemon on the side. Or make a simple Gremolata (page 198) and sprinkle it over the still-hot chicken, or a quick Lemon Salsa Verde (page 197) to serve on the side.

Lemons shoot life into fried food, mushroom soups, oysters. Your average supermarket strawberry has a better chance of tasting of something if you grate lemon zest over it. Imagine smoked salmon without a judicious squirt of lemon juice. A spritz of lemon seems to wake up the flavor in almost any food, much as salt does. There are few dishes where a little lemon is not welcome.

The incredible lemon preserves, decorates, and enlivens our food. It can be dried, pickled, grated, sliced, candied, or squeezed.

Taste

As a world-class seasoning ingredient, the lemon is third only to salt and pepper. Few other ingredients can enhance both sweet and savory dishes so well. Lemons can be present as a major ingredient (as in Lemon-and-Black-Pepper Fried Chicken, page 115) or as a simple squeeze of juice used to tune a dish's flavor just so.

Lemon brings out the best in other foods. It balances the fat in fried foods with its natural acidity. It's a great foil for sweetness and creaminess in all forms. A few drops heighten the flavor of sauces and intensify the natural taste of fish. But it is its characteristic freshness more than any other quality that makes lemon indispensable. From a squeeze of juice over warm asparagus, grilled shrimp, or lamb kebabs to a sprinkling of zest over braised veal shanks, lemon makes everything taste fresher.

Lemon can be either best actress or best supporting actress, main event or sideshow. A larger quantity of lemon juice or zest naturally produces a dominant lemon flavor. Just a small amount will act as a catalyst for other flavors. Lemons can be used with the most delicate tastes, such as fish or chicken, where they support the flavor, or with pronounced tastes, such as lamb or onion, where they come into their own, delightfully altering the other familiar flavors. Lemons have a unique ability to complement and enhance other foods and flavors. Sometimes you won't even detect the lemon flavor, but you notice there is something delightful and fresh about a dish.

Lemons are essential for desserts. Their acidity balances the oversweet, brings out the flavors of some fruits, and prevents the discoloration of others. But they are equally useful as an ingredient in their own right. Use them as a principal flavoring for desserts when a balance of richness and piquancy is needed. Tart lemon juice is the perfect complement to the sweetness of sugar. Because of their acidity, lemons are wonderful in baking. Their tart flavor overcomes the sometimes too "eggy" nature of cakes, custards, and soufflés. They can lift and reveal the flavors in a fruit dessert, and mingle with and heighten its aroma.

Lemons in the Kitchen

In the world outside the kitchen, "a lemon" refers to a dud. Not so in the kitchen. Think of the best cooks you know: chances are they are never without fresh lemons. For centuries, cooks all over the world have found ways to use lemons.

While some people rave about the flavor and juiciness of California's Meyer lemons, or the tart lemons of Sicily or Menton, France, even the ordinary American supermarket variety lemon is quite wonderful.

When you cook with lemons, you can count on fragrance. Nothing smells as good in the kitchen as lemons, from lemon meringue pie to chicken roasted with lemons.

Lemons are naturally beautiful at every stage of their lives. In the orchard, they radiate beauty. If you walk through a grove of lemon trees at dusk, you will see the fruit glowing like lanterns among the dark green leaves, an experience surpassed only by walking through the groves at blossom time, when the scent is unbelievably powerful and heady.

After they make their way to the stores, whatever the season—sizzling heat or crisp frost—lemons piled high in shops and markets are a wonderful sight, with their clean, sharp color. Even when they are set among far rarer, more exotic beauties, they hold their own.

Once home, placed in a cobalt blue bowl in the kitchen, lemons are just as beautiful as, and far less expensive than, fresh-cut flowers. After the lemon has decorated your kitchen for a day or so, you will cut that lemon and add gorgeous lemon slices as pretty garnishes to a wide range of sweet and savory dishes. Brightly colored lemons shimmering in your marmalade are as inviting as it gets. Lemons never disappoint.

all about *lemons*

The versatile lemon plays an integral role in the culinary process—
the skin, seeds, juice, and flesh all contribute in their own right and collectively
to the chemistry of food. The lemon activates change—
it is the revolutionary of the food world.

—CHRISTINE MANFIELD, *Paramount Cooking*

Buying Lemons

Whether you are buying your lemons at a farm stand or a supermarket, you don't have to worry about ripeness. Every lemon in the market is fully ripe and ready to use, so you can pick and choose according to what you'll be using them for.

If you're looking for juice, choose firm but not rock-hard lemons that are heavy for their size. Very hard ones invariably yield little juice. Slightly softer, medium-sized, and thin-skinned lemons are juicier. Heaviness indicates that lemons are fresh and full of juice; heft them and compare to find the weightiest fruit.

If you're looking for zest, thicker-skinned lemons usually have more abundant, flavorful zest and are easier to grate.

Lemons should be as bright as the sunshine, with a glossy sheen, a firmness to the touch, finely textured skin, and a pleasant citrus fragrance. The condition of the skin is important. A very coarse exterior may indicate an excessively thick skin, which in turn may mean less flesh and juice. Lemons should be vibrant, bright, and uniform in color, with unbroken skin, free of moist or brittle spots or shriveling. The fruit beneath the skin should feel firm, with no evidence of softness.

A small, very green stem is a sign of freshness. Lemons from warmer climates may have slightly

the tree and the fruit

The lemon tree is quite beautiful and can bear fruit every day of the year, frequently bearing fruit and blossoms simultaneously. It becomes fully productive around its tenth year and an average tree can yield 1,500 lemons a year, although some trees have been known to yield twice that amount.

The lemon tree reaches 10 to 20 feet in height and is a spiny tree with long irregular branches that usually have sharp thorns on the twigs. The pointed oblong leaves, reddish when young, become dark green above, light green below, and are from 2¹/₂ to 4¹/₂ inches long. The wonderfully aromatic large flowers may be solitary or there may be two or more clustered. The buds are reddish and the opened flowers have four or five petals, each about 3/4 inch long, that are white on the inside and purplish beneath, with twenty to forty stamens with yellow anthers.

Most lemon trees begin with the planting of seeds in the nursery. The young seedlings are the rootstock. When about two or three years old, the seedlings are budded—a bud is selected and cut from a mature lemon tree producing the type of lemon desired and slipped in a T-shaped cut made in the bark of the seedling. Tape holds the bud in place until it starts to grow. Soon the bud begins to grow into a leafy shoot. To help it grow straight, it is

green skin—it does not mean they are not ripe. But fruits that have a slightly greenish cast are likely to be more acidic than those that are a deep yellow. Deep yellow lemons are usually more mature than lighter yellow ones, and not quite as acidic.

Avoid lemons that are hard and rigid; they may have been frost-damaged. Also avoid lemons that are soft, spongy, wrinkled, or have bumpy, rough, or hard skin. A dark yellow or dull color or hardened or shriveled skin indicates old age. Soft spots, mold, or broken skin indicate decay, but brownish spots or patches may have been caused when branches rubbed against the immature fruit and are not a sign of damage.

Dampness is a great enemy to lemons. It's best not to buy lemons that have been displayed on ice or sprinkled with water in the store. Damp lemons will deteriorate quickly if they touch one another; mold, which spreads rapidly, will form and the lemons will soften and rot. That's why lemons used to be packed in boxes lined with sawdust—to absorb the moisture. (I remember when each lemon was wrapped in a twist of tissue paper to keep the damp away from the fruit.) And lemons are never picked in the morning, for the same reason; if the fruit is damp with the morning dew, it will deteriorate quickly.

You'll also want to stay away from lemons that have been stored near fruits with strong odors or ethylene-gas-producing fruits, such as apples. Pitting of the skin, that tinge of red interior discoloration, and loss of juice are all indications of a chill injury, when the fruit is damaged by cold temperature.

If you are going to use the peel, don't buy lemons that have been colored. Almost all of our lemons come from California and Arizona, neither of which allows lemon growers to color their fruit. If possible, check the box the fruit came in to see if the telltale words "color added" are there. You can't always tell a dyed lemon by looking at the skin, but sometimes you can: often a red dye that doesn't completely cover the greenish skin is used. As always, it pays to buy from a greengrocer you trust, one who knows if the fruit has been colored and will tell you so.

The primary varieties of commercially available lemons are the Lisbon and Eureka from California, Arizona, Chile, and Spain. Those grown in the U.S. are given one of four grades: U.S. #1, U.S. Export #1, U.S. Combination, and U.S. #2. The difference in grades relates primarily to appearance, mostly size. Organic lemons are becoming increasingly available.

Storing Lemons

Lemons store well, and they keep longer than any other citrus fruit. They are picked according to size, rather than ripeness, and are then placed in large temperature- and humidity-controlled rooms to "cure," or ripen. They are often kept this way for up to six months.

If you maintain similar storage conditions, you can keep lemons for quite a long time. Just remember that they like the same kind of tempera-

tied to the trunk of the seedling. When the bud is growing well, the seedling is cut off just above the place where the bud was attached. In about a year, this new young tree can be transplanted to a lemon grove. Lemons ripen 7 to 8 months after the flowers bloom.

Most citrus trees consist of two parts. The upper framework, called the scion, is one kind of citrus, and the roots and trunk, called the rootstock, are another. The place where the two parts come together, a barely discernible horizontal line around the trunk of a mature tree, is called the bud union. In Florida, most orange trees have lemon roots. In California, nearly all lemon trees are grown on orange roots. This sort of thing is not unique with citrus. With stone fruits, there is a certain latitude. Plums can be grown on cherry trees and apricots on peach trees, but a one-to-one relationship like that is only the beginning with citrus. A single citrus tree can be turned into a carnival, with lemons, limes, grapefruit, tangerines, kumquats, and oranges all ripening on its branches at the same time.

—John McPhee, *Oranges*

The ideal storage conditions for lemons are temperatures from 58° to 60°F with 89 to 91 percent relative humidity. A USDA test revealed that stored that way, lemons lost weight at the rate of only 2 to 3 percent per month; that juice content of the individual lemons actually increased the first month; and that the ascorbic acid concentration remained nearly constant throughout 7 months of storage.

ture for storage as they do for growing, not too warm and not too humid—the proverbial cool, dry place. Lemons will keep at room temperature for up to 2 weeks and in the refrigerator for as long as 6 weeks. Be extra careful with them in humid weather, even more so than in the heat; humid conditions will make them rot quickly. Your refrigerator's vegetable bin is always best for long-term storage. Some authorities recommend storing refrigerated lemons immersed in water in a jar with a tight-fitting lid, to prevent loss of moisture, and they may last even longer that way. If you want to store lemons at room temperature, keep them in a cool room on a tray or in an open basket so that air can circulate around them, and turn them over now and then to make sure that they are not getting moldy (one moldy lemon will ruin the rest very quickly). Whether in or out of the refrigerator, lemons should not be stored in plastic, which encourages moistness and mold.

Whole lemons should never be frozen; the juice sacs burst, and when the fruit thaws, the pulp may be dry and mushy. But both lemon zest and juice freeze well. If you have more lemons on hand than you can use before they are likely to spoil, remove the zest and juice them, then freeze each separately. Or, if you don't remove the zest, the juiced shells can be frozen to use as containers for sauces, sorbets or other desserts, or relishes.

Freeze freshly grated lemon zest or strips of zest removed with a vegetable peeler in small self-sealing plastic bags for up to 3 months. You'll have it ready to add flavor and aroma to your meals anytime. You can freeze freshly squeezed lemon juice for up to 4 months. Many cooks prefer to freeze the juice in ice cube trays, 2 tablespoons per cube, rather than in larger quantities, so they don't have a big block of frozen juice. Then transfer the frozen cubes to plastic bags. Fresh lemon juice can also be kept in the refrigerator, in a tightly covered container, for 2 to 3 days without significant loss of flavor.

Frozen lemon slices or wedges are great for adding to iced tea, lemonade, and many other drinks. Cut lemons into paper-thin slices or wedges, lay them on baking sheets, and freeze until solid. Then carefully remove them and transfer to a self-sealing plastic bag until you need them. Lemon twists can be frozen in the same way.

Always refrigerate a zested lemon and juice it within a few days, since the fruit quickly deteriorates without its protective skin. When you only need half a lemon, store the remaining half cut side down on a small plate in the refrigerator, and use it as soon as possible.

If some lemons do get away from you, don't use those past their prime for cooking. Their taste will have turned metallic and very unpleasant. Use them instead for polishing copper pans or for other household chores.

Lemon juice *is used as a fundamental seasoning, like salt or pepper. It adds a brightness to food. A squeeze of lemon on grilled meats will temper the richness and bring out the flavor.*

—Rocco DiSpirito
(chef-owner, Union Pacific, New York City)

Coarse nets *suspended in the storeroom are very useful for preserving lemons.*

—*The Practical Housekeeper* (1857)

lemon varieties

Ninety-five percent of the lemons produced for the fresh market in the United States are grown in California and Arizona. The crop is planted with two major varieties, Lisbon and Eureka. The fruits of the two varieties are so similar it is difficult for the average person to tell them apart. They differ only slightly in size, shape, and thickness of peel. Eureka lemons are distinguished by a short neck at the stem end; Lisbons have no distinct neck, but the blossom end tapers to a pointed nipple. Eurekas may have a few seeds and a somewhat pitted skin, while Lisbons are commonly seedless, with smoother skin. Both types have medium-thick skins and are abundantly juicy. Florida-grown lemons are likely to be a Lisbon-type called Bearss, with two s's. Although there are many varieties, they differ very little. It is often almost impossible to identify with certainty the fruit of a particular variety, since the range of different fruit shapes is often as wide from different flushes of the same tree as it is between varieties at the same time of year. With lemons, there are greater differences between the trees than between the fruits.

Deconstructing Lemons

Elliptically shaped lemons have a neck on the stem, or *peduncle,* end, and a nipple on the opposite, or *stylar,* end. There are three layers to the lemon's elegant structure. The thin colored outer layer is called the *epicarp,* also known as the zest or the rind. For culinary purposes, the zest is the bright yellow outer covering of the fruit and the peel is the whole of the skin, composed of both the zest and the pith attached to it. (In the fruit's immature state, the green pigment on the outside of the lemon is chlorophyll; as the fruit ripens, this gives rise to the yellow carotene.) Beneath the epicarp lies the *mesocarp,* or, commonly, the pith. This white connective tissue joining the peel to the pulp is nearly tasteless but bitter. It is the chief source of commercial grades of pectin, which is used to set jams and jellies and thicken shampoos.

The pulp, or *endocarp,* is the flesh of the fruit. The pulp of lemons, and most citrus fruits, is naturally divided into segments called *locules.* The juice is contained in *vesicles* that grow from hair-like tubes on the segment membranes. Within each vesicle are many juice cells, or *vacuoles.*

Lemon Juice

There are many ways to juice a lemon. Probably the simplest method is cutting it crosswise in half and inserting a fork while squeezing the lemon over a bowl to catch the juice. Or you might use a "reamer juicer," either manual or electric: simply a ribbed cone-shaped tool that releases the juice when the cut fruit is pressed down and rotated against it. Countertop pressers, with a rack-and-pinion gearing controlled by a lever or a handle, mean business. They exert hundreds of pounds of pressure on the lemon half to extract the maximum juice. Some are tall and others short, but you do need counter space for them. If you often juice many lemons, you might prefer an electric juicer, but you'll want a quiet one.

A "lemon trumpet," or "lemon faucet," available from kitchenware shops and through the Williams-Sonoma catalog (800-451-2233), allows you to extract a small amount of lemon juice without slicing the fruit. Simply twist it into the lemon and squeeze the fruit; the juice flows freely through the tube, and the seeds are strained out automatically. You can even store the lemon in the refrigerator with the trumpet still in place, until you need juice again. It's made of stainless steel and is dishwasher-safe.

Roll a room-temperature lemon on the counter a few times or drop it into hot water for a few minutes before you squeeze it—the lemon will give up its juice more easily.

When using lemon juice for baked goods, discard the seeds, of course, but don't strain out the pulp—it will add flavor and texture.

For maximum nutritional benefit, use freshly squeezed lemon juice immediately. Because vitamin C is a very volatile substance, most of this nutrient will be lost if you let the juice stand overnight, even if tightly covered. You can freeze

lemon juice, but it will lose nutritional value, just as the commercially frozen product does.

Bottled lemon juice can have a peculiar metallic undertaste, perhaps because it's the older, past-their-prime lemons that are processed. Always use freshly squeezed lemon juice, never the lemon juice sold in bottles or plastic containers.

Lemon Zest

For me, most of the joy of a lemon is in the zest. The juice is wonderfully refreshing and perfect for balancing flavors in a dish, but it's the aptly named zest that has an insistent lemon flavor. It's much more than just pretty packaging. Fragrant with aromatic natural oils, the zest imparts a freshness and a subtle yet lively layering of flavors whenever you use it. With its complex floral and tangy tastes as well as its slight, sophisticated bitterness, it heightens and accents other flavors.

If you wish to intensify the lemon flavor in a recipe, most often the thing to do is to add finely grated zest rather than more juice. The zest contains more flavor and will not affect the balance of the other ingredients. I find I almost always add a pinch of grated zest to a dish, even if initially I think I'll just use lemon juice; the zest underscores the citrus flavor and announces its presence both visually and texturally.

Zest can be used to brighten all kinds of dishes, sweet and savory, as a garnish, accent, or key ingredient. It adds a colorful counterpoint to fresh berry fillings, dried fruit compotes, suave custards, and creamy frostings. Mellowed when baked, it insinuates its sunny personality into cakes and cookies. A sprinkling of grated zest can brighten a rich stew, perk up a salad, or add zing to a stir-fry or vegetable sauté.

Always use fresh or frozen lemon zest, not dried (unless you dry your own; see page 15). Store-bought dried zest generally has lots of preservatives and little flavor.

A vividly colored peel is usually an indication of flavorful zest. Scratch the lemon with a finger-nail—the more fragrant the fruit, the more flavor-ful the zest.

Remember, overzealous grating will result in bitterness. What you want is only the thin yellow part of the skin. Precise measurement is crucial to the final balance of flavors, and that's especially true for lemon zest. Too much zest can also make a dish bitter. If you want to add more zest to a recipe, add it a little at a time, tasting after each addition.

Before zesting a lemon, wash it thoroughly. Fortunately, most of the insecticides used on commercially grown citrus fruits are washed off after harvesting. But after they are disinfected, they are coated with a water-soluble wax for protection during shipping. So lemons need to be washed thoroughly, even scrubbed with soap and warm water, to remove the wax. If you want to avoid pesticides completely, buy organic lemons, but they too should be washed thoroughly before using, as they are also usually coated with wax.

REMOVING LEMON ZEST

There are a number of tools that can be used for removing the zest from lemons. The one you use will be determined by how you plan to use the zest.

Graters   I used the Microplane grater for every recipe that calls for grated zest. A rasp, like those you would find in a carpenter's tool chest, it works better than any other implement for grating lemon zest. (The wife of a tool distributor, fed up with her dull kitchen grater, used one of her husband's rasps instead, and the Microplane was born.) The Microplane's razor-sharp teeth shave instead of ripping and shredding, and it removes a lot more zest than other graters and gadgets; you'll get at least a tablespoon of zest from each large lemon. It also seems never to remove the white pith, which is a minor miracle in itself. I love the larger model that has a molded rubber handle; it's very comfortable to hold and use and is well balanced, like a good knife. Just stroke the lemon across the Microplane—as if you were play-ing the violin—and you'll have fine, fluffy wisps of zest that are easy to collect and measure. It's easier to grate lemons if you draw them diagonally across the grater rather than up and down. The Microplane is made of stainless steel, easy to clean, and dishwasher-safe. For information on the Microplane grater, call 800-555-2767 or go to www.microplane.com. It's also available through

The Baker's Catalogue (800-827-6836) and in many kitchenware shops. It's the one "must have" tool for lemon lovers.

A box grater is great for shredding cheese, but lousy for lemon zest, as it tends to keep a good bit of the zest for itself and you have to dig for it inside. The side with the tiniest holes, the one known as the "knuckle mangler," always removes some of the bitter pith with the peel, and it compacts the fine shreds, so you may end up with more zest than you want. If you must use a box grater, use the side with the small tear-drop–shaped holes.

Vegetable Peeler   To remove wide strips of zest to infuse sugar syrups or flavor custards, drinks, marinades, and other dishes, use a sharp swivel-blade vegetable peeler. The peeler removes the zest easily and most will yield 10 to 12 strips per lemon, each about 2 inches long and ½ inch wide. Some vegetable peelers are sharper than others and some remove a thicker strip than others. I have one that's great for removing zest and another that fails miserably; it takes lots of the white pith with the zest. Be sure to scrape away any pith you accidentally remove with a small sharp knife. Crush or twist strips of zest just before using them to release the fragrant oils. Use the strips as is or cut them into fine shreds, depending on the recipe. For thinner strips, stack two or three and, using a very sharp knife, cut them lengthwise into needle-thin strips.

tips for zesting

- If you'll be using both the juice and the zest of a lemon, remove the zest first.

- The lemon's volatile oils are the strongest just after zesting, so always remove the zest just before using.

- Grate lemon zest over wax paper to make gathering it for measuring easier. To measure the grated zest, place it lightly in the measuring spoon.

- Finely grated zest adds more flavor than larger strips.

- The zest of a lemon need never be wasted. Even if your recipe only calls for the juice, remove the zest (either grated or in strips made with a vegetable peeler) and freeze in a tightly covered container for up to 3 months, or put it in a jar with sugar.

Before the invention of lemon zesters, Hannah Glasse, in *The Art of Cookery Made Plain and Simple* (1747), recommended grating lemon skins with a piece of broken glass.

Zester   A zester is a unique five-holed tool custom-made for citrus. It removes only the zest, none of the pith, in thread-like strips that are perfect as a garnish. A good-quality zester (available in kitchenware shops and some supermarkets) is an easy way to get very long, thin strands of lemon zest. I recommend the Oxo brand zester; the blade is at the perfect angle so it removes the finest and longest pieces, and it's very comfortable to use.

Press firmly (but not so firmly as to remove any of the bitter white pith) as you draw the zester down the lemon and stop pressing when the strips are as long as you want them to be. A zester is easy to clean and relatively inexpensive. If you use it in place of a grater, you will get less zest from the lemon.

Channel Knife   A channel knife is a handheld tool with a notched, usually stainless-steel, blade that cuts ¼-inch-wide strips of lemon peel. You can use it to remove the perfect martini twist or to notch a lemon before cutting it into beautiful slices that look like a daisy. You can also remove the peel in one continuous strip, beginning at one end and spiraling around the fruit. The channel knife produces a thick strip of peel, not just the zest like a vegetable peeler, which is great for garnishing. You can twist it decoratively and even tie it into a knot.

PRESERVING LEMON ZEST

Drying concentrates the aromatic oil in lemon zest, and dried zest is wonderful added to hot drinks, soups, or stews.

Dried Grated Lemon Zest   You can easily dry grated lemon zest just by placing it on a paper towel in warm place, such as the top of the refrigerator or a radiator. When it's completely dry, store it in small jars; it will keep for up to a month. For longer storage, you could freeze the dried zest, although you can freeze fresh zest just as well.

Oven-Dried Lemon Zest   If you want to keep a large quantity of dried zest on hand, dry it in the oven. To make a scant ½ cup: Preheat the oven to 175°F. Remove the zest from 4 lemons with a vegetable peeler. Place the strips of zest in a single layer, not touching one another, on a large baking sheet. Dry in the oven for 4 hours; let cool. Store the dried zest in a tightly sealed jar at room temperature. Use the strips of dried zest whole or grind in a spice grinder just before using.

nutritional information— one medium lemon

Lemons, powerful little nutrition packages, contain negligible fat and no cholesterol, are very low in sodium, and low in calories. Lemons have more vitamin C than any other citrus fruit.

Although other mammals are able to synthesize their own vitamin C internally, humans must obtain it from food sources. And because our bodies don't store this necessary vitamin, we must replenish it every day.

Calories 44
Protein 1.5 grams
Carbohydrate 12 grams
Fat 0.3 gram
Cholesterol 0
Sodium 3 milligrams
Potassium 200 milligrams
Iron 0.9 milligram
Calcium 66 milligrams
Vitamin A 30 International Units

PERCENT OF USRDA

Protein 3%
Vitamin A 0.2%
Vitamin C 120%
Calcium 2.5%

Cooking with Lemons

LEMON TIPS

˜ If a recipe calls for both lemon juice and zest, and they will be added at the same time, put the zest in a small bowl and pour the juice over the zest to keep it moist until you need it.

˜ For dishes that contain lemons or lemon juice, always use nonreactive cookware and containers such as stainless steel, enamel-coated cast iron, or plastic; avoid aluminum and uncoated cast iron or copper, which may discolor the food and impart an unpleasant metallic taste. Copper also quickly and completely destroys vitamin C.

˜ Use stainless-steel knives when cutting lemons; lemon juice reacts with carbon-steel knives, which can add a metallic taste.

˜ In order to retain the maximum amount of vitamin C in lemons and juice, avoid overcooking and high-heat cooking. Whenever possible, add lemon juice to dishes after they have been cooked, to preserve the vitamin C.

˜ Lemon juice "cooks" the flesh of seafood without heat, as in ceviche, the Peruvian classic, a boon on hot summer days.

˜ If you are cutting back on salt, add a spritz of lemon juice to almost any dish; the tart juice helps compensate for the missing salt.

˜ Fresh lemon juice can be substituted for vinegar in many recipes. Many gastronomes and wine connoisseurs use lemon juice instead of vinegar in salad dressings, because the lemon juice doesn't fight with the wine as much.

˜ Freshen poultry, after washing, by rubbing it with a cut lemon.

˜ Acidulating the water for poaching eggs with a few squeezes of fresh lemon juice helps keep the whites together and makes them a bright white.

˜ Lemon juice is a great addition to almost any marinade, not just for flavor but also for its ability to tenderize.

FRUITS AND VEGETABLES

˜ Lemons can be used as a short-term preservative. Their ascorbic acid acts as a natural antioxidant to prevent avocados, apples, bananas, pears, and other fruits that are prone to discoloration from oxidizing, or turning brown, when exposed to air after being cut.

- Throw a lemon half into the water when cooking cauliflower; it will both keep it white and help reduce cooking odors.

- Fresh lemon juice keeps mushrooms from turning an unpleasant dark color while they are cooking.

- Rinse grapes in a lemon-water solution to remove any mold or fungus.

SWEETS

- Need buttermilk for a recipe? Add a tablespoon of fresh lemon juice to a cup of milk and let it stand for 5 minutes until it curdles. You wouldn't want to drink it, but it's just right for a cake.

- Try adding a few drops of fresh lemon juice to whipping cream if it doesn't stiffen properly.

- Lemon juice turns royal icing a very bright white.

- A little lemon juice added to the poaching liquid for fruit helps keep it from breaking up or losing its shape.

- In older pie crust recipes, you'll often see lemon juice listed as an ingredient (usually only 1 or 2 teaspoons). Try it: the acid tempers the gluten in the dough, helping to achieve tenderness.

A few drops *of sour lemon juice can tweak us into a heightened awareness and appreciation of a myriad different flavors. Almost everything we eat contains at least a tiny amount of acid, or we would find it insipid.*
—Margaret Visser, *Much Depends on Dinner*

Using citrus *peel in cooking is like discovering bright red lipstick. It will change your life.*
—Barbara Tropp

- Try substituting a teaspoon of lemon juice for each ¼ teaspoon of cream of tartar in meringue recipes.

- To keep soft cookies soft, add a slice of lemon to the cookie jar.

- Even lemon seeds and pith are useful. They are richer than other citrus fruits in pectin, and commercial pectin, in fact, is derived from lemons. Instead of buying commercial pectin when making jams and jellies from low-acid fruits, such as strawberries and raspberries, add lemon pith and seeds, wrapped in cheesecloth, when you cook the fruits and sugar. (You can add the lemon pulp as well, as it is also rich in pectin, and the juice it releases will improve the flavor of whatever preserve you are making.) Fresh fruit preserves made without the addition of lemon juice are insipid.

- One large lemon will give you at least 1 tablespoon zest if you use a Microplane grater (see page 12), less if you use another type of grater.

- To peel a lemon, remove a thin slice from the top and the base of the lemon. Set the fruit on its base, and, with a small sharp knife, following the natural curve of the fruit, carefully cut down from the top to the bottom, removing both the rind and the pith in thick strips.

- To remove the sections, peel the fruit as described above. Slip a small sharp knife alongside the membranes on both sides of one section, freeing it, and let it fall into a bowl. Repeat with the remaining sections, removing the seeds as you go and reserving the juice. Squeeze the juice from the membranes over the sections. Cut the sections into smaller pieces if you wish.

LEMON BASICS

- A large lemon will give ¼ cup juice; a medium lemon will give about 3 tablespoons.

- For 1 cup juice, use 4 large or 5 to 6 medium lemons.

Gorgeous Garnishes

Garnishes should be fun and easy, and lemons make some of the simplest, tastiest, and most brightly colored garnishes around. Luscious and eye-catching, they can add a touch of glamour or a fun, lighthearted feel to a dish or drinks. A garnish should enhance the food's flavor and add color, as well as complement the texture of the other foods being served. A colorful garnish can be almost as important to a recipe as a key ingredient. Keeping it simple is usually best, although occasionally you may want something a little more elaborate.

A good sharp knife is important for making beautiful garnishes. A slicer of some kind often comes in very handy. A mandoline, the chef's tool, is terrific, but there are other less expensive and less complicated options. My favorite is the Feemster Slicer, also called an old-fashioned slaw cutter. It's a small slicer with a very sharp carbon-steel blade that is easily adjustable for the desired thickness. The Feemster has been around forever and is very inexpensive, under $10 in hardware stores and kitchenware shops.

Cartwheel Slices and Twists

Large lemons that have a thick layer of pith do not make attractive slices. Look for small, slightly rounded fruit with comparatively fine textured skin. When perfect thin slices are needed, chill the lemons first, and cut the slices from the center; use the ends for juicing. Lemon slices can be cut into a variety of shapes and used as a decoration for both sweet and savory dishes. They are also refreshing added to water, cool fruit juice, or many hot drinks, and they are indispensable in certain alcoholic drinks.

For cartwheel twists, cut through the peel to the center of the lemon slice and simply twist to make an S shape.

Decorated Slices

For cogwheel slices, also called fluted slices, use a channel knife (see page 14) to remove lengthwise strips of zest from the lemon, then thinly slice the lemon: hold the stem and blossom ends of the fruit between your thumb and middle finger and pull the channel knife through the peel from end to end, leaving about ⅜ inch between each cut. Cut the lemon into slices of the desired thickness; cut them in half for half-cogwheel slices, if desired.

Candied Lemon Slices

Lovely served with pork or duck or other poultry, or used as a garnish for desserts. See page 226 for the recipe.

Frozen Lemon Rounds

A terrific garnish for desserts, but also a refreshing treat to nibble on after a hearty meal. Slice lemons as thin as possible—about ⅛ inch thick—and discard the seeds. Lay out a sheet of plastic wrap on a baking sheet and arrange the lemon slices on it, not touching one another. Sprinkle the slices generously with sugar and freeze until hard. They will keep for up to a month in a self-sealing plastic bag in the freezer, although they might stick to each other.

Lemon Wedges

Wedges are really used for their juice, not their appearance, but they can certainly brighten a plate. They are most often served with seafood, poultry, lamb, and other savory dishes so that each diner can squeeze lemon juice to taste onto the food. To make wedges, cut a lemon lengthwise in half; place it cut side up and cut each half into 3 or 4 wedges. If you want to get fancy, dip the edges of lemon wedges in minced fresh herbs or in chile powder.

Lemon-Wedge Curls

Cut a lemon into 8 wedges. With your fingers, gently separate the peel from one end of the wedge, to about three-quarters of the way down. Tuck the tip of the peel under the fruit section. Use to garnish hot or cold seafood or iced drinks.

Lemon Squeezers

These are perfect for a dinner party, or anytime you don't want lemon seeds and lemon juice flying at the table. Cut a lemon crosswise in half. Make 2 stacks of two 6-inch squares of cheesecloth each. Place 1 lemon half, cut side down, in the center of each stack. Gather the edges of the cheesecloth together and tie with a length of string. Wrap the string around the bag and insert a sprig of the fresh herb of your choice under the string, if desired.

Grated Zest

If you use a Microplane (see page 12) rather than a box grater, you'll get more zest and less pith. Just rub the fruit firmly across the grater.

Zest from a Zester

Using long strokes, draw the zester firmly from the top to the bottom of the lemon. Each stroke will produce very thin strips of zest, leaving the white pith behind. See page 14 for more information on zesters.

Needle-Thin Strips of Zest

A pretty decoration for a variety of sweet and savory dishes. Remove the zest with a vegetable peeler; remove any white pith from the zest with a sharp paring knife. With a sharp knife, cut the strips lengthwise into very fine shreds. If you like, let the strips stand in a bowl of ice water until they curl. Scatter over caramelized oranges or use to decorate a cheesecake or a mousse.

Candied Julienne Strips of Zest

See page 229 for a simple recipe.

Lemon Twists

Lemon twists can be made with a vegetable peeler or with a special tool called a channel knife (see page 14). If using a vegetable peeler, remove 2-inch-long strips from the lemon; remove any pith with a sharp paring knife. A channel knife produces a perfect thin twist, just right for James Bond's martini; simply pull the tool down the peel of the fruit.

Lemon Spiral

Use a channel knife (see page 14) to cut a long spiral of peel from a lemon, but leave it attached to the lemon. Arrange it next to the fruit in an attractive way for a terrific decoration.

Lemon Shells

Cut a lemon lengthwise or crosswise in half and carefully juice the halves with a reamer. Scrape the shells clean with a spoon. To prevent tipping, cut a thin slice off the bottom of each shell. Refrigerate or freeze until ready to use, depending on how soon you will be using them and what you'll be using them for. Fill the chilled or frozen shells with ice cream, frozen yogurt, tartar sauce, relishes, or dressings.

Lemons are part *rind, part juice, part magic.*
—Sylvia Thompson

If *I were forced to give up every fruit in the world but one I would have absolutely no trouble choosing. The lemon wins, hands down.*
—Laurie Colwin, *More Home Cooking*

Lemon Stars
(also called the Vandyke Cut)

With a small sharp knife, cut a lemon in half in a zigzag pattern by making V cuts all the way around it, being sure to connect each new cut to the last one. Keep the cuts as straight as possible. Cut a small slice from the bottom of each lemon half so it will not tip over. Dip the cut sides in minced fresh parsley, if desired.

Lemon Chips

These are wonderful as a garnish for desserts and savory dishes, or for household decorations like wreaths. Cut lemons into ⅛-inch-thick slices, discarding the ends; do not seed. Place the slices on a large wire rack on a baking sheet and dry in a preheated 175°F oven for 4 hours. Remove from the oven and leave on the rack to air-dry for several hours, depending on the humidity.

To use as a garnish, stand a single slice in a serving of ice cream, sorbet, pudding, cake, or other dessert.

Deep-Fried Lemon Zest

This is a great garnish for a simple fish dish. To make about 2 tablespoons deep-fried zest, enough for 2 servings, remove the zest from 2 lemons with a zester. Halve the lemons and squeeze the juice into a small shallow bowl. Add the zest and ½ teaspoon salt, toss together, and let stand for 30 minutes.

Pour vegetable oil into a small deep saucepan to at least 2 inches deep and heat over medium-high heat to 375°F. (I use a digital Polder thermometer with a probe for the oil; it makes deep-frying in small batches very easy.) Drain the zest and pat dry between paper towels. Fry the zest, in two batches, for about 30 seconds; just as it begins to brown, begin to remove it with a slotted spoon. Be careful, as it burns quickly. Transfer the zest to paper towels to drain and use immediately.

Glazed Preserved Lemon

Remove and discard the pith from ¼ Preserved Lemon (page 218). Cut the peel into long needle-thin strips. Combine the zest with 3 tablespoons water, 1 tablespoon sugar, and a pinch of crumbled saffron threads in a small saucepan and simmer until translucent, 2 to 3 minutes. Remove the rind from the syrup and use as a garnish. This is especially good with fish.

Chocolate-Coated
Lemon Leaves

You'll need about 4 ounces bittersweet or semisweet chocolate to coat 20 lemon leaves. Wash the lemon leaves and dry thoroughly with paper towels. Melt the chocolate and let it cool until slightly thickened, about 5 minutes. With a table knife, spread a thick layer of chocolate on the underside of each leaf (the underside provides the best vein markings), to just short of the edges. Avoid getting chocolate on the front of the leaf; it will make removal difficult and make the chocolate leaves more likely to break. Refrigerate on a wax paper–lined wire rack for about 25 minutes, or until the chocolate is set. Hold the stem of each leaf and gently peel it away, touching the chocolate as little as possible. Refrigerate or freeze until firm, then put on a tray, cover, and refrigerate until ready to use.

appetizers

Lemon and Fennel Black Olives

for a change of pace, use half black Niçoise olives and half green Picholine olives here. Both are available in specialty foods stores and some supermarkets.

MAKES ABOUT 2 CUPS

2 cups brine-cured black Mediterranean olives (about 24 ounces)
2 tablespoons Lemon Oil (page 214) or olive oil
1 teaspoon fennel seeds, lightly crushed
1 teaspoon finely grated lemon zest
½ teaspoon coarsely ground black pepper

Stir together all of the ingredients in a bowl. Refrigerate, covered, for at least 1 day, and up to 2 weeks, before serving. Serve at room temperature.

Lemon, Coriander, and Garlic Green Olives

a favorite way to prepare olives in Cyprus, these olives are a grand combination of Mediterranean flavors.

MAKES ABOUT 2 CUPS

2 cups cracked green Mediterranean olives (about 24 ounces)
6 thin lemon slices, seeded
3 garlic cloves, crushed with the side of a chef's knife
2 tablespoons Lemon Oil (page 214) or olive oil
1 teaspoon coriander seeds, lightly crushed

Stir together all of the ingredients in a bowl. Refrigerate, covered, for at least 1 day, and up to 2 weeks, before serving. Serve at room temperature.

Black Olives with Lemon and Hot Red Pepper

i like to use large, luscious Kalamata olives for this recipe. If you don't have an olive bar at your local fancy food store, Krinos packs quite wonderful Kalamata olives in jars that are available in most supermarkets. I usually store these olives in self-sealing plastic bags in the refrigerator (as I do all of the olive recipes).

MAKES ABOUT 2 CUPS

**2 cups brine-cured black Mediterranean olives
   (about 24 ounces)
1 small sprig fresh rosemary
8 thin lemon slices, seeded and quartered
2 tablespoons Lemon Oil (page 214) or olive oil
1 garlic clove, halved
1 teaspoon crushed hot red pepper flakes**

Stir together all of the ingredients in a bowl. Refrigerate, covered, for at least 1 day, and up to 2 weeks, before serving. Serve at room temperature.

Green Olives with Preserved Lemons and Mint

using cracked olives allows the olives to absorb more of the added flavors. You could use flat-leaf parsley and/or cilantro instead of the mint.

MAKES ABOUT 2 CUPS

**2 cups cracked green Mediterranean olives
   (about 24 ounces)
2 tablespoons finely shredded fresh mint leaves
Peel of ¼ Preserved Lemon (page 218), cut into
   long thin strips
2 tablespoons juice from Preserved Lemons
   (page 218)
2 tablespoons Lemon Oil (page 214) or olive oil
2 garlic cloves, thinly sliced**

Stir together all of the ingredients in a bowl. Refrigerate, covered, for at least 1 day, and up to 1 week, before serving. Serve at room temperature.

Lemon-and-Coriander-Cured Salmon

for special occasions, cured salmon is a simple and elegant choice—festive, lovely to look at, and utterly delicious. It is also easy to prepare, though you do need to plan ahead. Make sure the skin of the salmon has been left on and all of the small bones are removed, or the salmon will be very difficult to slice. A 5-pound bag of sugar is perfect to use as the weight for the salmon; cans or bags of beans or rice also work well.

SERVES 4

2 lemons
One 1¼-pound salmon fillet, with skin
3 tablespoons sugar
3 tablespoons kosher salt
1 tablespoon cracked black peppercorns
1 tablespoon coriander seeds, lightly crushed
1 tablespoon Lemon Vodka (page 166) or vodka
Lemon-Cucumber Sandwiches (page 31) for
    serving, optional

1. Finely grate the zest from the lemons. Slice the lemons into thin slices and discard the seeds.

2. Trim any fat from the salmon. Run your finger gently over the fish, feeling for any small bones, and remove them with tweezers. Place the fish skin side down in an 8-inch square glass baking dish.

3. Stir together the lemon zest, sugar, salt, peppercorns, and coriander in a small bowl. Rub the lemon vodka over the top of the fish, coat with the lemon zest mixture, and lay the lemon slices on the fish. Cover the fish tightly with plastic wrap. Place a piece of cardboard cut slightly smaller than the dish on top, place a 5-pound weight on the cardboard, and refrigerate for 48 hours, turning the salmon 4 times.

4. When ready to serve, discard any liquid in the dish. Scrape off the lemon slices and most of the peppercorn mixture from the fish. Cut the salmon diagonally into very thin slices and arrange on a serving platter. Serve with Lemon-Cucumber Sandwiches, if desired.

Lemon Scallop Ceviche

Ceviche is originally from Peru, but it is popular throughout Latin America. The acid in the lemon actually "cooks" the scallops: the flesh becomes firm and they become opaque. Be sure your scallops are impeccably fresh. This is gorgeous served on a bed of radicchio.

SERVES 4 TO 6

1 pound tiny bay scallops
1 mild red onion, finely diced
1 yellow bell pepper, cored, seeded, and finely
   diced
Zest of 1 lemon, removed with a vegetable peeler
1 cup fresh lemon juice (about 4 large lemons)
1 cup loosely packed fresh cilantro leaves
3 tablespoons Lemon Oil (page 214) or olive oil
1 to 3 jalapeño chiles, seeded and minced
1 to 2 garlic cloves, mashed to a paste with
   ½ teaspoon salt
¼ teaspoon ground coriander
Radicchio leaves for serving, optional

1. Stir together all of the ingredients except the radicchio in a large bowl. Refrigerate, covered, for at least 4 hours, or until the scallops are opaque throughout and firm. The ceviche can be refrigerated for up to 24 hours.

2. Just before serving, taste and add more salt if necessary. Serve the ceviche chilled, on radicchio leaves, if desired.

Lemon-Cucumber Sandwiches

Lemon sandwiches on whole-grain bread are the classic accompaniment to smoked salmon in Britain. I like to serve them with Lemon-and-Coriander-Cured Salmon (page 29). But you don't need the cured salmon to serve these; if you want a tea sandwich with the refreshing flavor of lemon, here it is. (If you don't have a mandoline or Feemster slicer for cutting paper-thin slices of lemon, use just the cucumber, as too-thick lemon slices are very unpleasant.)

MAKES 16 TEA SANDWICHES

2 **Kirby cucumbers, cut into paper-thin slices**
Salt and freshly ground black pepper
4 **tablespoons (½ stick) unsalted butter, at room temperature**
1 **teaspoon finely grated lemon zest**
1 **teaspoon fresh lemon juice**
12 **paper-thin lemon slices, seeded**
8 **very thin slices homemade-style whole wheat or white bread (see Note)**

1. Place the cucumber slices in a colander, sprinkle with ½ teaspoon salt, and let drain for 15 minutes.

2. Stir together the butter, zest, lemon juice, and salt and pepper to taste in a small bowl.

3. Quickly rinse the cucumbers, drain, and pat dry on paper towels.

4. Cut 4 of the lemon slices in half. Spread each slice of bread with lemon butter. Top 4 of the slices with the cucumber slices. Arrange 2 whole lemon slices diagonally on each of these slices of bread, then fit 2 half-slices around the whole lemon slices. Top with the remaining bread and press the sandwiches gently together. Trim off the crusts, cut the sandwiches diagonally into quarters, and serve.

NOTE:
I use Pepperidge Farm thinly sliced bread.

Steak Tartare with Lemon and Capers

One theory is that this dish comes from the Tartars of the Russian Baltic provinces, who ate shredded raw meat. Always use the freshest and highest-quality beef available. Discard every bit of fat, and keep in mind that it's best if you chop it yourself, as close to serving time as possible.

SERVES 4

8 ounces beef tenderloin, fat trimmed and finely chopped or ground
1 shallot, finely chopped, plus additional finely chopped shallots for garnish
2 tablespoons finely chopped fresh flat-leaf parsley, plus additional for garnish
1 tablespoon drained capers, finely chopped, plus additional whole capers for garnish
1 large egg yolk, lightly beaten
1 teaspoon finely grated lemon zest
1½ teaspoons fresh lemon juice
1 teaspoon Dijon mustard
¼ teaspoon salt
Pinch of freshly ground black pepper
Warm toast for serving

1. Stir together the beef, shallot, parsley, capers, egg yolk, zest, lemon juice, mustard, salt, and pepper in a medium bowl just until blended.

2. Shape the mixture into 4 oval patties. Arrange them on a platter and garnish with finely chopped shallots, parsley, and capers. Serve with the warm toast.

Lemon and Thyme
Parmesan Biscuits

Use a Microplane grater (see page 12) for both the zest and the Parmesan cheese. Think of these as savory butter cookies, perfect before dinner, not after. They are best served warm and are lovely with a dry white wine. The dough can be made well ahead, placed in a self-sealing bag, and frozen until ready to thaw, slice, and bake.

MAKES ABOUT 40 BISCUITS

1 cup all-purpose flour
1½ teaspoons fresh thyme leaves
½ teaspoon salt
¼ teaspoon coarsely ground black pepper
8 tablespoons (1 stick) unsalted butter, at room
temperature
1 tablespoon finely grated lemon zest
2 cups finely grated Parmigiano-Reggiano
cheese (about 8 ounces)
½ cup toasted sliced almonds (see Note)

1. Stir together the flour, thyme, salt, and pepper in a small bowl.

2. With an electric mixer on medium-high speed, beat the butter and zest in a medium bowl until light and fluffy. Add the cheese in 4 batches, beating until well combined.

3. Add the flour mixture and beat on low speed just until combined; the dough will look very dry and will only come together when you press it together with your fingers. Stir in the almonds.

4. Divide the dough into 2 equal pieces. On a work surface, roll each piece under your palms into an 8-inch-long log. Wrap tightly and refrigerate for at least 30 minutes, and up to 2 days. The dough can be frozen for up to 2 months.

5. Position a rack in the middle of the oven. Preheat the oven to 350°F. Butter two large baking sheets.

6. Cut each log of dough into ⅜-inch-thick slices and arrange 1 inch apart on the baking sheets. Bake for 15 minutes, or until golden brown. Transfer the biscuits to wire racks to cool slightly.

NOTE:
Toast the almonds on a baking sheet in a 350°F oven for 7 to 10 minutes, or until golden brown.

Lemon-Ginger Garlic Bread

If you've already got your grill fired up, toss this on it—no reason to heat up your kitchen. You might consider sprinkling fresh parsley or cilantro leaves over the butter.

MAKES 1 LOAF

6 tablespoons (¾ stick) unsalted butter, at room temperature
1 tablespoon finely grated lemon zest
2 teaspoons finely minced peeled fresh ginger
1 garlic clove, mashed to a paste with ¼ teaspoon salt
Pinch of freshly ground black pepper
1 loaf French or Italian bread

1. Preheat the oven to 350°F.

2. Stir together the butter, zest, ginger, garlic paste, and pepper in a small bowl.

3. Split the loaf of bread lengthwise in half with a sharp serrated knife. Spread the butter mixture onto the cut sides of the bread and put the halves back together. Wrap the bread tightly in aluminum foil.

4. Bake the bread for 15 minutes, or until heated through. Unwrap, cut into thick slices, and serve hot.

Lemon and Fig Tapenade

This tapenade has a wonderful flavor, sweet and salty at the same time. Serve it with thin crisp toast and a soft mild goat cheese, such as Montrachet.

MAKES ABOUT 1 CUP

2 garlic cloves, peeled
2 dried Black Mission figs, stems discarded, quartered
2 to 4 anchovy fillets
1 cup brine-cured black Mediterranean olives, pitted
1 tablespoon drained capers
3 tablespoons Lemon Oil (page 214) or olive oil
1 tablespoon finely grated lemon zest
2 tablespoons fresh lemon juice
2 teaspoons Cognac or other brandy
Pinch of freshly ground black pepper

1. With the motor running, drop the garlic through the feed tube of a food processor and process until finely chopped. With the motor still running, add the figs and anchovies and process until finely chopped. Add the olives and capers and process until finely chopped.

2. Transfer to a bowl and stir in the lemon oil, zest, lemon juice, Cognac, and pepper. Serve immediately or refrigerate, covered, and bring to room temperature before serving.

adding lemon flavor

- Make smoked salmon tea sandwiches using Lemon Butter (page 182) and thinly sliced whole wheat bread. Or use paper-thin radish slices and fresh mint leaves instead of the salmon.

- Make a spread for croutons by pureeing cooked fresh fava beans, olive oil, lemon juice and zest, and fresh mint leaves.

- Add fresh lemon juice and finely grated zest to hummus.

- Add lemon zest and chopped fresh herbs to a soft mild goat cheese for a lovely spread for bread or crackers.

- Do as the Greeks do, and grill cheese on lemon leaves.

- Add finely grated lemon zest and fresh thyme leaves to deviled eggs.

- Toss blanched whole almonds with Lemon Oil (page 214) and roast until golden brown.

- Prepare marinated mushrooms using Lemon Oil (page 214) or olive oil, lots of lemon juice and zest, bay leaves, and fresh flat-leaf parsley.

- Top a focaccia with fresh rosemary leaves, golden raisins, and paper-thin lemon slices.

- Grill mozzarella crostini and top each with finely grated lemon zest and an anchovy fillet.

- Serve stuffed grape leaves with Avgolemono Sauce (page 190).

- Add lots of lemon juice and zest to your favorite homemade or store-bought baba ghanoush.

- Sprinkle hot oven-fried or deep-fried potato chips with Gremolata (page 198).

soups

Lemony Tomato Soup

this is my favorite tomato soup and I serve it year-round, either hot or cold. Pomi brand chopped tomatoes are as good as many fresh tomatoes, and they make this a very quick and easy pantry soup. Feel free to use flat-leaf parsley instead of the basil, especially in wintertime, when fresh basil is scarce.

MAKES ABOUT 4 CUPS

2 tablespoons unsalted butter
1 onion, chopped
1 stalk lemongrass, finely chopped, optional
1 garlic clove, chopped
One 26.45-ounce aseptic package chopped tomatoes or 1½ pounds ripe tomatoes, chopped
2 sprigs fresh basil, plus finely shredded fresh basil leaves for garnish
Finely grated zest of 2 lemons
2 teaspoons light brown sugar
1 teaspoon salt
¼ teaspoon freshly ground black pepper
2 to 3 tablespoons fresh lemon juice
Sour cream or plain yogurt for serving

1. Melt the butter in a large saucepan over medium heat. Add the onion, lemongrass, if using, and the garlic and cook, stirring occasionally, until softened, about 5 minutes. Add the tomatoes, 1 cup water, the basil sprigs, zest, sugar, salt, and pepper and bring just to a boil. Reduce the heat and simmer, covered, for 15 minutes.

2. Discard the basil sprigs. Puree the soup in a blender, in batches, and pour through a strainer. To serve hot, gently reheat in a clean saucepan. Or, to serve cold, let cool to room temperature, then refrigerate, covered, for several hours, or until thoroughly chilled.

3. Just before serving, stir the lemon juice into the soup. Serve garnished with the sour cream and shredded basil leaves.

sumac

Sumac is the ground or whole berries of an edible variety of sumac shrub. This spice has a tart, lemony flavor and was used in the Mediterranean region and the Middle East before the arrival of lemons from Europe. In Turkey, where it is called *sumak*, it is commonly served sprinkled on top of kebabs and as a tabletop condiment. It is available in Middle Eastern markets and specialty foods shops.

Classic Avgolemono Soup

This is served not just in Greece, where it is really a national dish, but also in Middle Eastern countries and parts of North Africa. It has a lush, smooth texture. Avgolemono is also good prepared with orzo pasta instead of rice. Garnish the soup with a pinch of ground sumac, if you'd like.

MAKES ABOUT 4 CUPS

4 cups chicken stock or canned low-sodium
    chicken broth
Zest of 2 small lemons, removed with a vegetable
    peeler
1 imported bay leaf or ½ California bay leaf
2 cardamom pods, crushed, 1 cinnamon stick,
    or a large pinch of crumbled saffron threads,
    optional
⅓ cup long-grain white rice
2 large eggs
1 large egg yolk
2 tablespoons fresh lemon juice
Salt
Cayenne pepper
Paper-thin lemon slices for garnish
Finely shredded fresh mint leaves or finely
    chopped fresh flat-leaf parsley for garnish
Pinch of ground sumac, optional

1. Combine the stock, zest, bay leaf, and cardamom, if using, in a large Dutch oven and bring to a boil over medium-high heat. Cover and boil for 5 minutes. Remove the zest, bay leaf, and cardamom pods with a slotted spoon, or pour the broth through a strainer and return to the pot.

2. Add the rice and return to a boil. Reduce the heat and simmer, covered, for about 17 minutes, or until the rice is just cooked through.

3. Meanwhile, whisk together the eggs, yolk, lemon juice, and salt and cayenne to taste in a medium bowl just until blended, not frothy.

4. Remove the Dutch oven from the heat. Slowly add ½ cup of the stock to the egg mixture, whisking constantly. Slowly pour the mixture back into the remaining stock, whisking constantly.

5. Cook, stirring constantly, over low heat until the soup is slightly thickened, about 5 minutes. Do not let it boil, or the eggs will scramble. Serve the soup hot, garnished with the lemon slices, mint, and optional sumac.

The clear sharp *tang of lemon was unknown to the ancient Greeks; this lovely fruit made its first appearance in Greece at the time of the thirteenth-century Crusades. But it would be difficult now to imagine Greece without its profusion of lemon trees, or a Greek meal without the color and piquant flavor lemons bring.*
—Rosemary Barron, *The Flavors of Greece*

Avgolemono Soup with Cod and Shrimp

If you prefer, use long-grain white rice instead of the orzo; it will take about 17 minutes to cook.

MAKES ABOUT 7 CUPS

1 pound medium shrimp, shelled and deveined (shells reserved)
Zest of 2 lemons, removed with a vegetable peeler
1 shallot, thinly sliced
1 imported bay leaf or ½ California bay leaf
2 garlic cloves, peeled
½ teaspoon fennel seeds
¼ teaspoon saffron threads, crumbled
⅓ cup orzo pasta
1 pound cod fillets
2 large eggs
1 large egg yolk
¼ cup fresh lemon juice
¾ teaspoon salt
Dash of hot red pepper sauce
Finely chopped fresh flat-leaf parsley for garnish

1. Combine 4 cups water, the reserved shrimp shells, the zest, shallot, bay leaf, garlic, fennel, and saffron in a medium saucepan and bring to a boil over high heat. Reduce the heat to low and simmer, covered, for 10 minutes.

2. Pour the liquid through a strainer into a large saucepan. Bring to a boil, add the orzo, and simmer for 12 minutes, or until the orzo is al dente.

3. Meanwhile, cut the cod fillets diagonally into strips about 2 inches long and ¼ inch thick.

4. Add the cod and shrimp to the broth and cook, stirring, until just cooked through and opaque throughout, about 5 minutes.

5. Meanwhile, whisk together the eggs, yolk, lemon juice, salt, and hot pepper sauce in a medium bowl just until blended, not frothy.

6. Remove the saucepan from the heat. Slowly add ½ cup of the broth to the egg mixture, whisking constantly. Slowly pour the mixture back into the remaining broth, stirring constantly.

7. Cook, stirring constantly, over low heat, until the soup is slightly thickened, about 5 minutes. Serve hot, garnished with parsley.

Thai Lemon and Coriander Soup

Iook for Mae Ploy brand Thai curry paste for this recipe. It comes in several types, often designated by color, such as red, green, or yellow. Available in Asian markets, it is inexpensive, lasts forever, and has tons of flavor. Be careful not to use too much; it is hot and spicy.

MAKES ABOUT 5 CUPS

4 cups chicken stock or canned low-sodium chicken broth
One 15-ounce can peeled straw mushrooms, rinsed and drained
2 teaspoons Thai red curry paste
½ skinless, boneless chicken breast, cut diagonally into long ⅜-inch-thick strips
2 tablespoons fresh lemon juice
¼ teaspoon salt
1 cup fresh cilantro leaves

1. Combine the stock and mushrooms in a large saucepan and bring to a boil over medium-high heat. Add the curry paste and boil, covered, for 5 minutes.

2. Remove the saucepan from the heat and add the chicken, lemon juice, and salt. Cover and let stand for 5 minutes, or until the chicken is cooked through.

3. Just before serving, stir in the cilantro.

 lemongrass

A pale yellow-green stalk of lemongrass resembles a tough old leek, but it has one of the freshest, cleanest flavors around. Lemongrass has a strong, sweet, citrusy taste and perfume, like a combination of lemon and an exotic flower. It's available fresh in many Asian markets and gourmet markets, usually with the root ends sitting in a tub of water. Avoid dried lemongrass, which has no flavor. Instead, freeze a few stalks of fresh lemongrass when you find it, so you will always have it on hand.

Lemony Chicken Broth

I often enjoy a mug of this fragrant broth on its own. It's great for making risotto or for adding lemon flavor to any of your favorite soups. You can use either a 48-ounce can of low-sodium chicken broth or your own homemade stock.

MAKES ABOUT 4 CUPS

1 tablespoon Lemon Oil (page 214) or vegetable oil
1 large shallot, thinly sliced
2 quarter-sized slices fresh ginger, optional
2 garlic cloves, peeled
6 cups chicken stock or canned low-sodium chicken broth
Zest of 1 lemon, removed with a vegetable peeler
4 black peppercorns
1 stalk fresh lemongrass, cut into 1-inch pieces, optional
2 tablespoons fresh lemon juice
Salt and freshly ground black pepper

1. Heat the lemon oil in a large saucepan over medium-low heat. Stir in the shallot, ginger, if using, and the garlic and cook, stirring, for 2 minutes. Add the chicken stock, zest, and peppercorns, increase the heat to high, and bring to a boil. Reduce the heat and simmer for 15 minutes. Add the lemongrass, if using, and simmer for 15 minutes longer.

2. Pour the broth through a strainer into a large glass measure or bowl. Add the lemon juice and season to taste with salt and pepper. Use the broth at once, or refrigerate for up to 2 days, or freeze for up to 3 months.

Zesty Summertime Garden Soup

make this chilled soup when your garden (or the farmers' market) is full of corn, tomatoes, and basil. You can garnish the soup with tiny sprigs of fresh basil or not.

MAKES ABOUT 7 CUPS

4 cups buttermilk (not unsalted)
2 cups seeded and chopped ripe tomatoes (about 2 large tomatoes)
2 cups fresh corn kernels (3 to 4 ears)
1 cup finely chopped fresh fennel or seeded English cucumber
18 fresh basil leaves, finely shredded, plus tiny sprigs fresh basil for garnish, optional
1½ teaspoons finely grated lemon zest
1 teaspoon salt
¼ teaspoon coarsely ground black pepper

1. Stir together the buttermilk, tomatoes, corn, fennel, basil, zest, salt, and pepper in a large bowl. Refrigerate, covered, for at least 2 hours, or until very cold, and up to 24 hours.

2. Serve the soup chilled, garnished with the basil sprigs, if desired.

adding lemon flavor

SOUPS

- Add grated lemon zest and chopped fresh herbs to yogurt, sour cream, or crème fraîche and use to garnish soups.

- Serve lemon wedges as a garnish for both cold and hot soups.

- Add a squeeze of lemon juice and float thin lemon slices in vegetable, beef, or chicken broth.

- Add lemon zest, saffron, and parsley to your favorite seafood chowder.

- Flavor a jellied consommé with lemon and the fresh herb of your choice—mint is lovely.

- Add lemon zest and snipped fresh chives to vichyssoise.

- Stir Gremolata (page 198) or Lemon Persillade (page 197) into minestrone or other vegetable soups just before serving.

salads and *salad dressings*

Potato Salad with Lemon and Parsley

this is perfect for a summertime BBQ or picnic. It goes with just about everything. The potatoes need to be really quite small, about 1½ inches in diameter. If yours aren't that size, cook them longer and then cut them into pieces.

SERVES 8

2¾ pounds very small red and/or white potatoes, scrubbed and quartered
¼ cup plus 2 tablespoons finely chopped fresh flat-leaf parsley
2 shallots, minced
1 tablespoon finely grated lemon zest
3 tablespoons Lemon Oil (page 214) or olive oil
2 tablespoons Lemon Vinegar (page 213) or seasoned rice vinegar
1 teaspoon salt
¼ teaspoon freshly ground black pepper

1. Bring the potatoes and enough salted water to cover to a boil in a large saucepan over high heat. Reduce the heat and simmer until the potatoes are tender when pierced with a fork, about 10 minutes. Drain.

2. Transfer the potatoes to a large bowl. Add the parsley, shallots, zest, lemon oil, lemon vinegar, salt, and pepper and stir gently to combine. Let stand for at least 10 minutes before serving.

3. Serve the salad warm, at room temperature, or slightly chilled.

Parsley Salad with
Lemon Vinaigrette

lemon and parsley may just be *the* best culinary combination. And here it is in a simply perfect salad, wonderful for a dinner party. You might serve it garnished with curls of Parmigiano-Reggiano cheese, removed with a vegetable peeler. I was introduced to parsley salad by James Beard many years ago, and the first time I tried it, I was hooked.

SERVES 6 TO 8

1 shallot, minced
1 teaspoon finely grated lemon zest
1 garlic clove, minced
2 tablespoons Lemon Vinegar (page 213) or
    seasoned rice vinegar
½ teaspoon Dijon mustard
¼ teaspoon salt
Pinch of freshly ground black pepper
¼ cup Lemon Oil (page 214) or olive oil
6 cups loosely packed fresh flat-leaf parsley leaves
    (about 2 bunches)
6 cups loosely packed fresh curly parsley leaves
    (about 2 bunches)
Parmigiano-Reggiano curls for garnish,
    optional

1. Whisk together the shallot, zest, garlic, vinegar, mustard, salt, and pepper in a small bowl. Whisking constantly, slowly add the lemon oil in a thin stream, and continue to whisk until the vinaigrette is smooth and emulsified.

2. Just before serving, toss the parsley with the dressing in a large bowl. Arrange the salad on a chilled serving platter or salad plates and serve immediately, garnished with Parmigiano-Reggiano curls, if using.

Baby Greens with
Broiled Lemons

I know someone introduced me to this salad, I just can't remember who it was. Thank you, whoever you are. It's great—warm, salty, sweet caramelized lemons topping chilled baby greens. Clean-tasting and refreshing, this salad is excellent for entertaining, but the lemons have to be prepared at the last minute.

SERVES 6

2 lemons, cut into paper-thin slices and seeded
2 tablespoons sugar
1 teaspoon salt
8 cups mixed baby greens, washed and spun dry
2 tablespoons Lemon Oil (page 214) or olive oil
¼ teaspoon freshly ground black pepper

1. Combine the lemons, sugar, and salt in a medium bowl and let stand for 1 hour, stirring occasionally.

2. Preheat the broiler. Place the lemons on a baking sheet in a single layer and spoon the liquid remaining in the bowl over them. Broil about 3 inches from the heat for 4 to 6 minutes, or until lightly browned, turning the pan if necessary so the lemons brown evenly.

3. Meanwhile, place the greens in a serving bowl.

4. Add the hot lemons and their liquid, the lemon oil, and pepper to the greens and toss to combine well. Serve immediately.

 meyer lemons

Aptly described as "all perfume, no pucker" by Amanda Hesser in the *New York Times,* Meyer lemons have a more delicate and more complex perfume than supermarket varieties. Aromatic with both floral and herbaceous overtones, and a sweet touch of lime, they seem sweeter than the common lemon, although in fact they do not contain more sugar, only less acid. They have a tight, smooth, very thin bright yellow skin that darkens to orange yellow as the fruit ripens. Rounder than the conventional lemon varieties, and practically seedless, Meyers are very juicy.

For the cook, Meyer lemons mean lemonade without sugar and being able to use the entire lemon in uncooked and cooked dishes. You can use them as you would an orange. Because they add a rounder edge and a mellowness to both sweet and savory dishes, Meyers are best used where true lemon sourness is not needed. One exception—they make extraordinary savory Preserved Lemons (page 218) and maybe even more stunning Sweet Preserved Lemons (page 225).

Look for Meyer lemons that have a bright daffodil-yellow skin and are firm but not hard. Softer lemons will yield lots of juice, but will be difficult to zest. Called "California's dooryard darlings," Meyers are more perishable than supermarket lemons, and their long bearing season makes them relatively difficult to harvest. They also need to go straight to market once picked, rather than be stored and ripened like supermarket

Meyer Lemon and Blood Orange Salad with Fennel

I adapted this from a recipe in Fran Gage's *Bread and Chocolate* (Sasquatch Books, 1999). Blood oranges are in season during late fall and winter and are available at produce markets and specialty food stores.

SERVES 6

1 fennel bulb, trimmed and thinly sliced
½ mild red onion, thinly sliced
2 Meyer lemons, peeled, thinly sliced, and seeded
Salt and freshly ground black pepper
1 tablespoon fresh Meyer lemon juice
3 tablespoons extra virgin olive oil
2 blood oranges, peeled, thinly sliced, and seeded

Combine the fennel, onion, lemons, and salt and pepper to taste in a medium bowl. Add the lemon juice and toss well, then toss with the olive oil. Add the oranges and toss gently, so they don't discolor the other ingredients. Serve immediately.

Lemony Tabbouleh

this is tabbouleh Middle-Eastern–style, with tons of parsley and just a little bulgur. You might add ½ teaspoon ground coriander and/or a pinch of ground allspice. It's best served the day it's prepared.

SERVES 4 TO 6

¼ cup bulgur wheat
4 small ripe tomatoes, seeded and finely chopped
1 cup finely chopped fresh flat-leaf parsley
1 bunch slender scallions, trimmed and finely chopped
2 tablespoons Lemon Oil (page 214) or olive oil
2 teaspoons finely grated lemon zest
2 tablespoons fresh lemon juice
2 tablespoons finely chopped fresh mint
1 garlic clove, mashed to a paste with 1 teaspoon salt
Pinch of cayenne pepper
Romaine lettuce leaves for serving, optional

1. Put the bulgur in a small bowl, add warm water to cover, and let soak for 15 minutes. Drain thoroughly in a strainer.

2. Combine the bulgur, tomatoes, parsley, scallions, lemon oil, zest, lemon juice, mint, garlic paste, and cayenne in a large bowl. Line a serving platter with romaine leaves, if using, arrange the tabbouleh on the platter, and serve.

varieties. And since they are too delicate to ship, so they aren't farmed commercially. If you live in California, look for them at farmers' markets (or on backyard trees). If you live in a large city, you may be able to purchase Meyer lemons at specialty foods stores or greengrocers, or you can mail-order them from Melissa's or Frieda's (addresses listed below). Store them in the refrigerator, where they will last for several weeks.

To make a heavenly sweet syrup to use for desserts, heat 1/2 cup water, 1/2 cup sugar, and 2 tablespoons finely grated Meyer lemon zest in a saucepan over medium heat, stirring until the sugar is dissolved. Simmer for 5 minutes. Let cool to room temperature, then strain. This will keep in the refrigerator for several weeks.

- **Frieda's**
  4465 Corporate Center Drive
  Los Alamitos, CA 90720
  (800) 241-1771
  www.friedas.com

- **Melissa's**
  P.O. Box 21127
  Los Angeles, CA 90021
  (800) 588-0151
  www.melissas.com

Middle Eastern–Style Orange and Lemon Salad

i love this refreshing salad and I think you will, too. I adapted it from a recipe in Sonya Uzvezian's wonderful book, *Recipes and Remembrances from an Eastern Mediterranean Kitchen* (University of Texas Press, 1999). You can vary the recipe as you want—try adding chopped preserved lemon peel, black Mediterranean olives, or minced garlic. This is perfect with grilled chicken.

SERVES 4

4 navel oranges
2 small lemons
½ teaspoon salt
Generous ¼ teaspoon ground cumin
Generous ¼ teaspoon ground coriander
¼ teaspoon cayenne pepper
½ small mild red onion, thinly sliced
8 fresh mint leaves, finely shredded
2 tablespoons Lemon Oil (page 214) or olive oil

1. Following the natural curve of the fruit, peel the oranges and lemons with a small sharp knife, removing all of the peel and pith in thick strips. Cut the oranges into thin crosswise slices and discard the seeds. Finely chop the lemon pulp and discard the seeds.

2. Arrange the orange slices on a deep platter and top with the chopped lemon. Sprinkle with the salt, cumin, coriander, and cayenne. Scatter the onion slices and mint over the top. Drizzle with the lemon oil and serve immediately, or refrigerate, covered, and serve slightly chilled.

Tomato Salad with Lemon and Basil

the combination of tomatoes and lemon is especially wonderful with basil, but feel free to use other herbs. You might try ⅓ cup mixed tarragon, parsley, mint, and cilantro. You could also use Lemon Vinegar (page 213) instead of the fresh lemon juice in the dressing.

SERVES 6 TO 8

1 tablespoon finely grated lemon zest
2 tablespoons fresh lemon juice
2 garlic cloves, mashed to a paste with ½
    teaspoon salt
1 teaspoon Dijon mustard
1 teaspoon sugar
¼ teaspoon freshly ground black pepper
¼ cup Lemon Oil (page 214) or olive oil
6 ripe medium red, yellow, and/or orange
    tomatoes (about 3 pounds), cut
    crosswise into ½-inch-thick slices
1 small mild red onion, thinly sliced into rings
1 shallot, thinly sliced into rings
10 fresh basil leaves, finely shredded, for garnish

1. Whisk together the zest, lemon juice, garlic paste, mustard, sugar, and pepper in a small bowl. Whisking constantly, slowly add the lemon oil in a thin stream, and continue to whisk until the vinaigrette is smooth and emulsified.

2. Arrange the tomato slices on a deep platter. Sprinkle with the onion and shallot rings and pour the dressing over the salad. Let stand at room temperature for at least 30 minutes, and up to 1 hour, before serving. (Or cover and refrigerate for several hours; let come to room temperature before serving.)

3. Sprinkle the basil over the salad and serve.

Lentil and Lemon Salad

The tiny green lentils from France are ideal for this salad, but if brown ones are what you have, it will still be delicious. Smoked mozzarella (about 6 ounces, cut into ½-inch pieces) would also be good in this, or try adding thin slices of garlic sausage or finely shredded smoked chicken breast.

SERVES 6 TO 8

1½ cups green or brown lentils, picked over
    and rinsed
1½ teaspoons salt
1 mild red onion, thinly sliced
1 orange bell pepper, roasted, peeled, seeded,
    and cut into ½-inch pieces
1 yellow bell pepper, roasted, peeled, seeded,
    and cut into ½-inch pieces
¾ cup finely chopped fresh flat-leaf parsley
¼ cup plus 2 tablespoons Lemon Oil (page 214)
    or olive oil
1 tablespoon finely grated lemon zest
¼ cup fresh lemon juice
¼ teaspoon freshly ground black pepper
Romaine lettuce leaves for serving,
    optional
1 ripe tomato, seeded and chopped,
    for garnish
Lemon wedges for serving

1. Bring 6 cups water to a boil in a large saucepan over high heat. Add the lentils and return to a boil, then reduce the heat and simmer for 10 minutes. Add ¼ teaspoon of the salt and simmer until the lentils are just cooked through, about 10 minutes longer. Place the onion in a colander and drain the lentils in the colander. Transfer the lentils and onion to a large bowl.

2. Stir in the roasted peppers, parsley, lemon oil, zest, lemon juice, the remaining 1¼ teaspoons salt, and the pepper. Serve immediately, or let cool to room temperature, cover, and chill until ready to serve.

3. To serve, arrange the romaine leaves, if using, on a serving platter. Top with the lentils and tomato, and arrange the lemon wedges on the side. Serve the salad warm, at room temperature, or slightly chilled.

Salad Dressings

Creamy Lemon Vinaigrette

Superb on a simple green salad. Add a pinch of sugar if this is too tart for you. Or, for an herbed vinaigrette, add 1 teaspoon of minced fresh tarragon leaves.

MAKES ABOUT 1 CUP

¼ cup crème fraîche or sour cream
1 shallot, minced
1 tablespoon finely grated lemon zest
2 teaspoons fresh lemon juice
½ teaspoon Dijon mustard
1 teaspoon salt
¼ teaspoon freshly ground pepper, preferably
    white
¼ cup plus 1 tablespoon Lemon Oil (page 214)
    or olive oil

1. Whisk together the crème fraîche, shallot, zest, lemon juice, mustard, salt, and pepper in a small bowl.

2. Whisking constantly, slowly add the lemon oil in a thin stream, and continue to whisk until the vinaigrette is smooth and emulsified. Store in the refrigerator for up to 3 days, and shake or whisk well before using.

- Finely grated lemon zest

- Finely chopped Classic Moroccan-Style Preserved Lemon peel (page 218)

- Chopped drained green peppercorns packed in brine

- Minced fresh or roasted garlic

- Gremolata (page 198) or Cooked Gremolata (page 199)

- Gremolata Salt (page 210)

- Lemon Pepper (page 211)

- Lemon Honey (page 224)

- Chopped drained capers

- Finely chopped fresh flat-leaf parsley, basil, rosemary, thyme, mint, chives, cilantro, sage, tarragon, and/or shiso leaves

- Toasted sesame seeds

- Minced peeled fresh ginger

- Ground coriander

- Ground cumin

Basic Lemon Vinaigrette

here's my standard, all-purpose vinaigrette. See the sidebars for a list of all sorts of other goodies you might choose to add. You could also use walnut, hazelnut, pistachio, pinenut, or toasted peanut oil instead of the lemon oil.

MAKES ABOUT ¾ CUP

1 small shallot, minced
3 tablespoons fresh lemon juice
1 teaspoon Dijon mustard
1 teaspoon salt
Pinch of freshly ground black pepper
½ cup Lemon Oil (page 214) or olive oil

1. Whisk together the shallot, lemon juice, mustard, salt, and pepper in a small bowl.

2. Whisking constantly, slowly add the lemon oil in a thin stream, and continue to whisk until the vinaigrette is smooth and emulsified. Store in the refrigerator for up to 1 week, and shake or whisk well before using.

Preserved Lemon Vinaigrette

I like this best on romaine lettuce, but you may prefer it on a spinach salad.

MAKES ABOUT ¾ CUP

1 shallot, minced
2 tablespoons fresh lemon juice or Lemon
**   Vinegar (page 213)**
1 tablespoon minced peel of Preserved Lemons
**   (page 218)**
1 tablespoon juice from Preserved Lemons
**   (page 218)**
½ teaspoon Dijon mustard
Freshly ground black pepper
½ cup Lemon Oil (page 214) or olive oil

1. Whisk together the shallot, fresh lemon juice, lemon peel, preserved lemon juice, mustard, and pepper to taste in a small bowl.

2. Whisking constantly, slowly add the lemon oil in a thin stream, and continue to whisk until the vinaigrette is smooth and emulsified. Store in the refrigerator for up to 1 week, and shake or whisk well before using.

- Ground fennel or anise seeds
- Curry powder
- Minced anchovies or anchovy paste
- Mustard seeds
- Poppy seeds
- Nigella seeds
- Pinch of crumbled saffron threads
- Lemon Dust (page 212)
- Coarse-grain mustard
- Lemon Persillade (page 197)
- Chermoula (page 200)

 shiso

Shiso is a member of the mint family. Available fresh in many Asian markets, it's a large flat-leafed herb with an aromatic flavor resembling a combination of mint, basil, and cinnamon. Store it refrigerated for up to 1 week.

nigella seeds

Nigella seeds are used as a spice in Egypt, the Middle East, India, Turkey, and occasionally in Europe. A small black seed with an aromatic peppery flavor, they can be sprinkled on bread and used to flavor cakes, vegetables, stir-fried dishes, and pickles.

Soy and Sesame Oil Lemon Vinaigrette

give this a try on simple watercress salad, or for a special occasion, a mix of watercress and pea shoots.

MAKES ABOUT 1 CUP

¼ cup fresh lemon juice
2 tablespoons soy sauce
1 garlic clove, mashed to a paste with
    ½ teaspoon salt
1 teaspoon Asian sesame oil
½ teaspoon freshly ground black
    pepper
¾ cup Lemon Oil (page 214), grapeseed
    oil, or vegetable oil

1. Combine the lemon juice, soy sauce, garlic paste, sesame oil, and pepper in a blender.

2. With the motor running on low speed, add the lemon oil in a thin stream, blending until the vinaigrette is smooth and emulsified. Store in the refrigerator for up to 1 week, and shake or whisk well before using.

adding lemon flavor

SALADS AND SALAD DRESSINGS

- Blend equal amounts of fresh lemon juice and sugar and add a pinch of lemon zest; drizzle over fruit salad.

- Make a cherry tomato salad with finely shredded fresh mint leaves and finely grated lemon zest; add Basic Lemon Vinaigrette (page 58) and toss to coat.

- Add fresh lemon juice and a large pinch of zest to chicken, shrimp, egg, or tuna salad.

- Stir together thinly sliced mushrooms, a dollop of mascarpone cheese, lemon zest, and lots of coarsely ground pepper for a simple but superb salad.

- Make a white bean salad seasoned with Gremolata (page 198); add cooked shrimp, if you like.

- Make a chickpea salad with lemon juice and zest, chopped cilantro, and minced fresh ginger.

- Like black bean salad? Add finely grated lemon zest, finely diced red onion, crumbled feta cheese, and finely shredded fresh mint leaves to cooked or rinsed and drained canned beans, and stir together with a bit of Basic Lemon Vinaigrette (page 58).

- Add finely grated lemon zest to your favorite Caesar salad dressing.

- Make a salad of thinly sliced oranges and lemons with chopped fresh fennel, chopped black Mediterranean olives, and cilantro.

- Add finely grated lemon zest and a dab of anchovy paste to your favorite potato salad.

- Toss very thinly sliced mushrooms with Basic Lemon Vinaigrette (page 58) and top the salad with Parmigiano-Reggiano shavings (made with a vegetable peeler).

- Slice ripe red and yellow tomatoes and dress with Basic Lemon Vinaigrette (page 58) flavored with minced lemongrass.

- Roast cubes of winter squash until tender, then toss with Basic Lemon Vinaigrette (page 58), lemon zest, fresh thyme, and caraway seeds. Serve hot, at room temperature, or chilled.

- Grate carrots and radishes and dress with a lemon juice, zest, and honey dressing spiced with cinnamon.

- Serve roasted red and orange peppers with Gremolata (page 198) and finely chopped black Mediterranean olives.

- Make a broccoli salad flavored with anchovy, lemon zest, and mustard seeds.

- Finely shred peeled raw beets and toss with Basic Lemon Vinaigrette (page 58); garnish with a tiny sprinkle of Lemon Dust (page 212).

vegetables

Roasted Artichokes
with Lemon

I love artichokes, but boiled or steamed artichokes are often waterlogged, and the butter I dip the leaves in just runs right off—since butter and water don't mix. This recipe solves the problem. Roasting also intensifies and concentrates the flavor of the artichokes, and covering the roasting pan allows them to absorb all the flavors of the olive oil, lemon slices, and garlic. Add a minced fresh herb (thyme is good) with the salt and pepper if you'd like, but I think this is simply perfect as is.

SERVES 6

3 large artichokes
¼ cup Lemon Oil (page 214) or olive oil
¼ teaspoon salt
Pinch of freshly ground black pepper
6 lemon slices, seeded
3 garlic cloves, halved
2 tablespoons fresh lemon juice

1. Preheat the oven to 375°F.

2. Pull off and discard any small outer artichoke leaves. Cut off the thorny tips from the tops with a knife. Cut off the remaining tips with scissors. Cut the artichokes lengthwise in half and trim any coarse fibers from the stems and artichoke bottoms. Rinse and drain.

3. Pour the lemon oil into a 9 X 13-inch glass baking dish and stir in the salt and pepper. Roll the artichoke halves in the oil to coat and turn them cut sides down. Lift up each artichoke slightly and slip a lemon slice and a half garlic clove under each one. Tightly cover the baking dish with aluminum foil.

4. Bake for about 45 minutes, or until the artichokes are tender when pierced with a paring knife. Transfer the artichokes to a platter or serving plates, cut side up, and top each with a lemon slice and a half garlic clove.

5. Whisk the lemon juice into the liquid remaining in the baking dish and spoon over the artichokes. Serve hot or at room temperature.

Asparagus with Luscious Lemon Sauce

*f*or a terrific first course, place a poached egg on each serving of asparagus, then spoon on the lemony sauce. If you use larger asparagus, peel the stalks and cook longer, if necessary.

SERVES 4 TO 6

**2 pounds pencil-thin asparagus, tough
     ends trimmed**
⅓ cup crème fraîche
**2 tablespoons unsalted butter, at room
     temperature**
2 teaspoons fresh lemon juice
¼ teaspoon salt
Dash of hot red pepper sauce

1. Spread the asparagus in a steamer rack, all facing in one direction. Place over simmering water, cover, and steam for about 5 minutes, or until tender when pierced with a fork. Drain and pat dry on paper towels.

2. Meanwhile, bring the crème fraîche to a boil in a small saucepan over medium-high heat. Stir in the butter, lemon juice, salt, and hot pepper sauce, and return to a boil.

3. Arrange the asparagus on a serving platter and spoon the warm sauce over it. Serve immediately.

Green Beans with Lemon and Mint

*t*his is the perfect side dish for almost any warm-weather meal. It's very tasty and unusually refreshing.

SERVES 6

1 pound green and/or yellow wax beans
¼ cup packed fresh flat-leaf parsley leaves
¼ cup packed fresh mint leaves
1 teaspoon finely grated lemon zest
2 tablespoons fresh lemon juice
2 tablespoons Lemon Oil (page 214) or olive oil
1 teaspoon salt
¼ teaspoon freshly ground black pepper

1. Cook the beans in a large pot of boiling salted water until crisp-tender, about 5 minutes. Drain, refresh under cold running water to stop the cooking, and drain again; pat dry on paper towels.

2. Meanwhile, chop together the parsley, mint, and zest. Transfer to a serving bowl and stir in the lemon juice, lemon oil, salt, and pepper.

3. Add the beans to the bowl and toss with the parsley mixture. Serve at room temperature.

Grilled Eggplant with
Lemon and Mint

If you'd like, grill the eggplant outdoors over medium coals for about the same amount of time. Either way, this is lovely served as is or on a bed of arugula (you'll need one large bunch).

SERVES 4 TO 6

2 small ripe tomatoes, seeded and chopped
1 tablespoon finely shredded fresh mint leaves
1 tablespoon Lemon Oil (page 214) or olive oil, plus additional for grilling
1 teaspoon finely grated lemon zest
1 teaspoon fresh lemon juice
Salt and freshly ground black pepper
1 small eggplant, cut crosswise into eight ½-inch-thick slices

1. Stir together the tomatoes, mint, lemon oil, zest, lemon juice, ¼ teaspoon salt, and a pinch of pepper in a small bowl.

2. Heat a lightly oiled ridged grill pan over medium heat until hot but not smoking. Meanwhile, brush one side of each eggplant slice generously with lemon oil and season with salt and pepper.

3. Working in batches if necessary, place the eggplant oiled side down in the grill pan and cook for 3 minutes. Brush the slices with lemon oil, season with salt and pepper, turn, and cook until browned and cooked through, about 5 minutes longer.

4. Arrange the eggplant on a serving platter and top each slice with some of the tomato mixture.

Sautéed Mushrooms

This classic French technique brings out the mushrooms' meaty texture, the lemon freshens and heightens their flavor, and the acid in the lemon juice prevents them from turning dark as they cook. You could use shiitake mushrooms; discard the stems, and adjust the cooking time as necessary.

SERVES 4

2 tablespoons unsalted butter
1 large shallot, finely chopped
1 pound small white mushrooms, thinly
    sliced
1 tablespoon fresh lemon juice
¾ teaspoon fresh thyme leaves
¼ teaspoon salt
Pinch of freshly ground black pepper
1 tablespoon finely chopped fresh flat-leaf
    parsley
1 teaspoon finely grated lemon zest

1. Melt the butter in a large skillet over medium heat. Add the shallot and cook, stirring until softened, 3 minutes. Stir in the mushrooms, lemon juice, thyme, salt, and pepper and cook, stirring often, until the mushrooms are softened, about 5 minutes. Increase the heat to medium-high and cook, stirring, until most of the liquid has evaporated, about 3 minutes.

2. Remove the skillet from the heat and stir in the parsley and zest. Serve hot.

Lemony Baby Carrots

here's a great basic recipe. You might try varying it by adding minced fresh parsley, thyme, cilantro, a pinch of Chinese 5-spice powder, toasted sesame seeds, minced fresh ginger, or scallion lengths.

SERVES 4

One 16-ounce bag peeled baby carrots
1 tablespoon unsalted butter, Lemon Oil
    (page 214), or olive oil
2 teaspoons finely grated lemon zest
2 teaspoons fresh lemon juice
¼ teaspoon salt
Pinch of freshly ground black pepper

1. Cook the carrots in a large pot of boiling salted water until crisp-tender, 3 to 4 minutes. Drain in a colander.

2. Meanwhile, melt the butter in a large skillet over medium heat. Remove the pan from the heat and stir in the zest, lemon juice, salt, and pepper.

3. Return the skillet to medium-high heat, add the carrots, and toss until well coated and hot. Serve.

Sugar Snap Peas with Mint Gremolata

a perfect match with a roast leg of lamb for a springtime supper.

SERVES 4

1 pound sugar snap peas
1 tablespoon unsalted butter
1 garlic clove, minced
¼ teaspoon salt
Pinch of freshly ground black pepper
1 tablespoon finely shredded fresh mint leaves
1 teaspoon finely grated lemon zest

1. Cook the sugar snap peas in a large pot of boiling salted water until crisp-tender, 2 minutes. Drain in a colander, rinse under cold running water to stop the cooking, and drain again.

2. Heat the butter, garlic, salt, and pepper in a large skillet over medium heat until the butter melts. Add the sugar snap peas and cook, stirring, until heated through, about 2 minutes. Remove the skillet from the heat, stir in the mint and the zest and serve hot.

Fresh Lemon
Corn Custard

This delectable fresh corn pudding is a perfect side dish to serve when corn is at its best. You might add a small sprig of fresh basil to the milk mixture while it's steeping.

SERVES 8

1¾ cups milk

1 tablespoon finely grated lemon zest

¼ cup heavy cream

2 cups fresh corn kernels (about 4 ears)

2 tablespoons unsalted butter, at room temperature

2 tablespoons all-purpose flour

2 tablespoons sugar

¾ teaspoon salt

¼ teaspoon ground coriander

⅛ teaspoon cayenne pepper

3 large eggs

1. Preheat the oven to 325°F. Lightly butter an 8-inch square glass baking dish. Put on a kettle of water for the water bath.

2. Combine the milk and zest in a medium saucepan and bring to a boil over medium-high heat. Remove the saucepan from the heat, cover, and let stand for 5 minutes.

3. Pour the milk through a strainer into a glass measure or bowl and add the cream. Let cool to room temperature.

4. Bring a large saucepan of salted water to a boil. Add the corn, return the water to a boil, and boil the corn until tender, about 2 minutes. Drain the corn and pat dry on paper towels.

5. With an electric mixer on medium speed, beat the butter, flour, sugar, salt, coriander, and cayenne in a medium bowl, scraping down the sides of the bowl occasionally, until smooth, about 2 minutes. Add the eggs one at a time, beating well after each addition. Add the milk mixture and beat on low speed just until smooth. Stir in the corn.

6. Transfer the mixture to the prepared baking dish. Place the dish in a 9 X 12-inch baking pan, place the baking pan in the oven, and pour enough boiling water into the baking pan to come halfway up the sides of the baking dish.

7. Bake the custard for 45 to 55 minutes, or until the top is lightly browned and a knife inserted in the center comes out clean. Serve hot.

Spinach with Lemon and Golden Raisins

Use your largest skillet here. If you don't have a really big one, you may want to use a large pot. And consider using tongs; they work very well for tossing and turning the spinach. Serve this with roast chicken and mashed potatoes. You can also add a little or a lot of fresh basil, cilantro, and/or parsley leaves along with the spinach leaves.

SERVES 2

2 tablespoons unsalted butter
2 tablespoons golden raisins, chopped
1 tablespoon finely grated lemon zest
1 garlic clove, crushed with the side of a chef's
    knife
One 10-ounce package fresh spinach, large stems
    discarded and thoroughly washed
¼ teaspoon salt
Pinch of freshly ground black pepper

1. Melt the butter in a large skillet over medium heat. Stir in the raisins, zest, and garlic and cook, stirring, for 2 minutes. Stir in the spinach, salt, and pepper, increase the heat to high, and cook, turning the leaves, until they wilt and are tender, 2 to 3 minutes. Remove from the heat and discard the garlic.

2. Transfer the spinach to serving plates with a slotted spoon. Serve hot.

Turnips with Lemony Bread Crumbs

*f*eel free to use this crumb mixture on other blanched vegetables. It's great on cauliflower. I always make my bread crumbs in the food processor. You'll need less than one slice of bread for this recipe. It's best to have the vegetables in a single layer in the skillet, so use the largest one you have: a 12-inch pan is perfect.

SERVES 4 TO 6

8 small turnips (about 1½ pounds), peeled
2 tablespoons unsalted butter
¼ cup fresh bread crumbs
2 teaspoons finely grated lemon zest
¼ teaspoon salt
Pinch of freshly ground black pepper
1 tablespoon finely chopped fresh flat-leaf parsley

1. Bring a large pot of salted water to a boil. Add the turnips, return to a boil, and boil until tender when pierced with a fork, about 15 minutes. Drain in a colander. When cool enough to handle, cut each turnip into 8 wedges.

2. Melt the butter in a large skillet over medium-high heat. Add the turnips and cook, stirring occasionally, until they are golden brown on the edges, about 10 minutes. Stir in the bread crumbs, zest, salt, and pepper and cook, stirring, until the bread crumbs are browned, about 2 minutes. Stir in the parsley and serve hot.

Lemony Potato Gratin

think of these as uptown scalloped potatoes. They're wonderful for a dinner party or a holiday meal, everything a festive dish should be— soothing, simple, and very delicious.

SERVES 8

3 pounds baking potatoes, peeled and cut into ¾-inch pieces
2 garlic cloves, peeled
½ cup heavy cream
Zest of 2 lemons, removed with a vegetable peeler
¾ cup freshly grated Parmigiano-Reggiano cheese
¼ cup snipped fresh chives and/or finely chopped fresh flat-leaf parsley
2 tablespoons unsalted butter, at room temperature
½ teaspoon salt
¼ teaspoon freshly ground black pepper

1. Combine the potatoes, garlic, and enough salted water to cover in a large saucepan and bring to a boil over high heat. Reduce the heat and simmer until the potatoes are tender when pierced with a fork, about 15 minutes. Drain in a colander.

2. Meanwhile, bring the cream and zest just to a boil in a small saucepan. Remove the pan from the heat and let stand, covered, for 10 minutes.

3. Pass the potato mixture through a ricer or the medium disk of a food mill into a bowl. Pour the cream through a strainer into the potatoes and stir in ¼ cup of the Parmigiano-Reggiano, the chives, butter, salt, and pepper.

4. Preheat the broiler. Transfer the potato mixture to a 2-quart shallow flameproof baking dish or a 10-inch cast-iron skillet. Sprinkle the remaining ½ cup cheese over the top. Broil 2 to 3 inches from the heat source for 5 to 7 minutes, or until the top is golden brown and crusty. Serve hot.

Parchment-Baked Potatoes
with Mint and Lemon

Serve these as part of a warm-weather dinner, with tomato salad, corn on the cob, and crab cakes or grilled chicken. Use tarragon instead of mint, if you prefer.

SERVES 4

**3 tablespoons unsalted butter, melted and
    cooled**
1 shallot, minced
2 tablespoons finely shredded fresh mint leaves
1 teaspoon finely grated lemon zest
Salt and freshly ground black pepper
**1 pound tiny red potatoes, scrubbed and
    dried**

1. Preheat the oven to 350°F.

2. Stir together the butter, shallot, mint, zest, and salt and pepper to taste in a medium bowl.

3. Slice the potatoes as thin as possible. Add them to the butter mixture and gently stir to coat.

4. Cut 4 rectangles of parchment paper or foil, each about 8 X 14 inches. Fold each piece crosswise in half and, with scissors, trim the unfolded sides of each piece to form a half-heart shape. Unfold the hearts and divide the potatoes among them, arranging the potatoes just to one side of the fold line on each. Fold the other halves of the papers over the potatoes. Beginning at a folded corner, twist and fold the edges of each paper over to form tightly sealed packets, and seal the ends tightly by twisting them.

5. Place the packets on a baking sheet and bake for 17 minutes. Serve the potatoes in the packets, and slit them open carefully at the table.

Fresh Basil and Lemon Mashed Potatoes

Scrumptious served with roast chicken, fish, or pork, or as part of an all-vegetable dinner.

SERVES 6

6 medium baking potatoes, peeled and cut
    into ¾-inch pieces
2 large sprigs fresh basil, plus ¼ cup slivered
    fresh basil leaves
Zest of 2 lemons, removed with a vegetable
    peeler
6 garlic cloves, peeled
¼ cup Lemon Oil (page 214) or olive oil
2 tablespoons fresh lemon juice
2 tablespoons unsalted butter, at room
    temperature
½ teaspoon coarsely ground black pepper
Salt

1. Combine the potatoes, basil sprigs, zest, garlic, and enough salted water to cover in a large saucepan and bring to a boil over high heat. Reduce the heat to low, cover, and simmer until the potatoes are tender when pierced with a fork, 10 to 15 minutes. Drain the potatoes in a colander. Discard the basil sprigs and lemon zest.

2. Pass the potato mixture through a ricer or the medium disk of a food mill into a bowl. Stir in the lemon oil, lemon juice, butter, pepper, and salt to taste until well combined. Sprinkle the slivered basil over the potatoes and serve hot.

Roast Sweet Potatoes with Gremolata

here sweet potatoes are cut into wedges, like steak fries. (How long they are is not so important, although the longer they are, the better they look.) Thickness is what affects the cooking time, and since they won't all be exactly the same size, some will cook faster than others. Spread them out on the baking sheets in a single layer so they won't steam. I like mine dark brown.

SERVES 4

¼ cup Lemon Oil (page 214) or olive oil
2 pounds sweet potatoes, peeled and cut
    lengthwise into wedges about ¾ inch thick
1 tablespoon finely chopped fresh flat-leaf
    parsley
1 teaspoon finely grated lemon zest
1 small garlic clove, minced
¼ teaspoon salt
Pinch of freshly ground black pepper

1. Preheat the oven to 450°F.

2. Divide the lemon oil evenly between two large baking sheets and heat the pans in the oven for 5 minutes.

3. Add the sweet potatoes to the pans, gently stir to coat them with the hot oil, and spread them out in a single layer, without touching one another. Roast, shaking the pans and turning the potatoes every 10 minutes, for 30 to 40 minutes, until browned and crisp.

4. Meanwhile, make the gremolata: Chop together the parsley, zest, and garlic until finely minced and well combined.

5. Drain the potatoes briefly on paper towels, then carefully transfer to a platter. Season with salt and pepper and sprinkle with the gremolata. Serve hot.

adding lemon flavor

VEGETABLES

- Toss roasted cauliflower florets with chopped orange and lemon sections, honey, and lemon juice. Add your favorite herb, if desired.

- Squeeze a wedge of lemon over corn, carrots, summer squash, or potatoes after cooking and add a sprinkle of chopped scallions or fresh chives.

- Sauté spinach with garlic, anchovies, and lemon zest.

- Squeeze fresh lemon juice over steamed or boiled potatoes, or other vegetables, before you toss them with butter and fresh herbs.

- When you fry onion rings, fry thinly sliced lemons and small sprigs of fresh flat-leaf parsley along with them.

- Grill ripe tomato halves and gently toss with Basic Lemon Vinaigrette (page 58), with added lemon zest and finely shredded fresh basil leaves, while they're still hot.

- Stir a puree of sautéed parsley and finely grated lemon zest into your mashed potatoes—they'll be a gorgeous green.

- Add lots of lemon zest to your next batch of latkes, and consider serving them with applesauce flavored with lemongrass.

- Cook bitter greens in Lemon Oil (page 214) and serve lemon wedges alongside.

- Roast acorn squash halves with butter, lemon zest, and minced fresh ginger in the cavity.

- Top roasted asparagus with toasted sesame seeds and lemon zest.

- Toss cooked shredded Brussels sprouts with lemon zest and poppy seeds.

- Stir-fry blanched cauliflower florets with lemon zest, julienne strips of fresh ginger, and toasted sesame seeds.

- Grill ears of corn on the cob and serve with Lemon Butter (page 182).

- Grill eggplant slices and top with Lemon Salsa Verde (page 197).

- Gently simmer tiny peas with a pinch of lemon zest and just a sprinkling of finely shredded fresh tarragon leaves.

- Top cooked cauliflower with toasted bread crumbs and Gremolata (page 198).

- Add lemon zest and some soft mild goat cheese to leftover mashed potatoes and make great potato pancakes.

- Add crumbled saffron threads and strips of lemon zest to the cooking water the next time you make mashed potatoes.

- Roast potatoes with sprigs of oregano and serve with lemon wedges.

- When you make your favorite scalloped potatoes, steep lemon zest and a fresh herb such as thyme in the cream before using it.

grains, pasta, and *beans*

Simply Perfect Lemon and Parsley Couscous

If you don't have a preserved lemon on hand, use 3 strips of lemon zest, removed with a vegetable peeler and cut into needle-thin long strips. I like whole wheat couscous best, but if you prefer regular couscous, just follow the cooking directions on the package. You might also stir in a sprinkling of finely shredded fresh mint leaves, toasted pine nuts, and/or chopped seeded ripe tomato.

SERVES 4 TO 6

1½ cups Lemony Chicken Broth (page 44), canned low-sodium chicken broth, or water
1 cinnamon stick
4 cardamom pods, lightly crushed
1 cup whole wheat couscous
Peel of ¼ Preserved Lemon (page 218), finely chopped
½ cup finely chopped fresh flat-leaf parsley
Salt and freshly ground black pepper

1. Combine the broth, cinnamon, and cardamom in a large saucepan and bring to a boil over high heat. Stir in the couscous and preserved lemon and return to a boil. Reduce the heat, cover, and simmer until the liquid has been absorbed, about 2 minutes. Remove the pan from the heat and stir in the parsley and salt and pepper to taste. Let stand, covered, for 5 minutes.

2. Discard the cinnamon stick and cardamom pods and serve the couscous hot or at room temperature.

Fennel and Green Olive Risotto

You could use Lemony Chicken Broth (page 44), prepared without the lemongrass or ginger here, and in that case, you wouldn't need to add the zest, but add the juice either way. The flavors in this risotto are subtle and soft, so be careful not to add too much pepper.

SERVES 4

4 cups chicken stock or canned low-sodium chicken broth
1 large fennel bulb, trimmed and finely chopped, fronds reserved
Zest of 1 lemon, removed with a vegetable peeler
8 sprigs fresh flat-leaf parsley, plus 3 tablespoons finely chopped parsley
¼ cup Lemon Oil (page 214) or olive oil
2 shallots, finely chopped
1 garlic clove, thinly sliced
1 cup Arborio or Carnaroli rice
¼ cup dry white wine or dry vermouth
⅓ cup finely chopped pitted green Mediterranean olives
Salt and freshly ground black pepper
¼ cup freshly grated Parmigiano-Reggiano cheese
1 to 2 teaspoons fresh lemon juice

1. Combine the stock, reserved fennel fronds, the zest, and parsley sprigs in a medium saucepan and bring to a boil over high heat. Reduce the heat, cover, and simmer for 10 minutes. Remove the fennel fronds, zest, and parsley sprigs with a slotted spoon, or pour the stock through a strainer and return it to the saucepan. Keep the stock at a bare simmer.

2. Meanwhile, heat the lemon oil in a medium saucepan over medium-low heat. Add the chopped fennel, shallots, and garlic and cook, stirring, until softened, about 10 minutes; don't let the mixture brown. Increase the heat to medium, stir in the rice, and cook, stirring, until the edges of the rice become translucent, about 4 minutes. Add the wine and cook, stirring, just until the wine is absorbed.

3. Add about ½ cup of the simmering stock and cook, stirring frequently, until it is absorbed. Continue adding the stock about ½ cup at a time, stirring frequently, letting each addition be absorbed before adding the next, until the rice is al dente, 20 to 25 minutes; add the olives and salt and pepper to taste after the first 15 minutes.

4. Remove the pan from the heat and stir in the chopped parsley, the Parmigiano-Reggiano, and lemon juice to taste. Serve immediately.

Orzo
with Tiny Peas

a bit like a risotto prepared with orzo, this is a very versatile side dish. Use a 14½-ounce can of broth and frozen peas if you like. You can substitute 1 teaspoon fresh thyme leaves for the parsley.

SERVES 4 TO 6

2 cups Lemony Chicken Broth (page 44), canned low-sodium chicken broth, or water

1 cup orzo

3 tablespoons unsalted butter

1 large shallot, finely chopped

1 tablespoon finely grated lemon zest

2 cups tiny fresh peas or one 10-ounce package frozen tiny peas, thawed

½ cup freshly grated Parmigiano-Reggiano cheese

3 tablespoons finely chopped fresh flat-leaf parsley

1 tablespoon fresh lemon juice

Salt

¼ teaspoon freshly ground black pepper

1. Bring the broth and ½ cup water to a boil in a large saucepan over high heat. Stir in the orzo, reduce the heat to low, and simmer, partially covered, until the orzo is al dente and almost all the liquid is absorbed, about 14 minutes.

2. Meanwhile, melt the butter in a medium skillet over medium heat. Stir in the shallot and zest and cook, stirring frequently, until softened, about 2 minutes. Add the peas and cook, stirring, until bright green, about 2 minutes. Remove from the heat.

3. Sprinkle the Parmigiano-Reggiano over the orzo and stir until creamy. Add the peas, parsley, lemon juice, salt to taste, and pepper. Toss gently, transfer to a serving dish, and serve hot.

Creamy Lemon Fettuccine

really simple and really good. This is a classic; vary it however you'd like. You might top the pasta with 4 ounces of salmon caviar, julienned smoked salmon, or blanched asparagus tips. And you might use finely chopped fresh flat-leaf parsley instead of the chives.

SERVES 6 TO 8

1 cup heavy cream
2 tablespoons finely grated lemon zest
1 pound dried fettuccine
2 tablespoons unsalted butter
½ teaspoon salt
Pinch of freshly ground black pepper
2 tablespoons snipped fresh chives

1. Bring the cream just to a boil in a medium saucepan over medium-high heat. Remove the saucepan from the heat, add the zest, and let stand, covered, for 10 minutes. Pour through a strainer into a glass measure or bowl.

2. Meanwhile, cook the fettuccine in a large pot of boiling salted water according to the package directions, or until al dente. Drain in a colander, rinse with hot water, and drain again.

3. Add the butter to the pasta pot and melt over medium heat. Add the pasta, cream, salt, and pepper and toss to coat the pasta. Increase the heat to medium-high and bring the sauce to a boil, tossing gently. Cook, stirring constantly, until almost all the cream is absorbed, 4 to 5 minutes. Serve immediately, topped with the chives.

Penne with No-Cook Tomato Sauce, Lemon, and Herbs

this perfect summer dish can sit at room temperature for up to 6 hours before serving. It's best not to refrigerate it: cold temperatures don't do anything good for tomatoes. If you're serving this as a side dish, use less mozzarella—about 4 ounces—or leave it out entirely. The dish is delightful even without it.

SERVES 4 TO 6

2 pounds ripe tomatoes, seeded and chopped
   (about 3 cups)
⅓ cup Lemon Oil (page 214) or olive oil
1 small mild red onion, cut into ¼-inch dice
¼ cup finely chopped fresh herbs (see Note)
1 tablespoon finely grated lemon zest
1 garlic clove, mashed to a paste with 1
   teaspoon salt
¼ teaspoon freshly ground black pepper
1 pound penne
12 ounces fresh mozzarella, cut into ½-inch dice

1. Stir together the tomatoes, lemon oil, onion, herbs, zest, garlic paste, and pepper in a medium bowl. Set aside at room temperature.

2. Cook the pasta in a large pot of boiling salted water according to the package directions, or until al dente. Drain in a colander.

3. To serve hot or warm, immediately toss the pasta with the mozzarella in a large bowl until the cheese is slightly melted, then add the tomato mixture. To serve later at room temperature, toss the hot pasta with the tomato sauce and let cool, then add the mozzarella; set aside, covered, at room temperature until ready to serve.

NOTE:
When choosing your herbs, if using tarragon, be sure to use only a small amount, 1 or 2 teaspoons at most—otherwise, it will overwhelm the other herbs. The perfect ratio would be about 1 tablespoon each finely chopped mint, basil, parsley, and snipped chives with a teaspoon or so of tarragon. Or use just one of these four herbs, omitting the tarragon.

Spaghetti with Whole-Tomato Sauce

Refreshing and clean-tasting, this dish is especially good hot and spicy, so add even more pepper flakes if you'd like.

SERVES 4 TO 6

1 pound spaghetti
⅓ cup Lemon Oil (page 214) or olive oil
1 cup finely chopped shallots (about 4 large shallots)
2 garlic cloves, thinly sliced
Zest of 2 lemons, removed with a vegetable peeler and cut lengthwise into needle-thin strips
½ cup finely chopped fresh flat-leaf parsley
⅓ cup finely shredded fresh basil leaves
2 tablespoons finely shredded fresh mint leaves
¾ teaspoon salt
¼ to ½ teaspoon crushed hot red pepper flakes
One 35-ounce can whole Italian plum tomatoes, drained
Freshly grated Parmigiano-Reggiano cheese for serving

1. Cook the spaghetti in a large pot of boiling salted water according to the package directions, or until al dente. Drain in a colander.

2. Meanwhile, heat the lemon oil in a large deep skillet over medium heat until hot but not smoking. Add the shallots, garlic, and zest and cook, stirring, until the shallots are softened, about 5 minutes. Stir in the parsley, basil, mint, salt, and pepper flakes and cook, stirring, for 2 minutes. Stir in the whole tomatoes and cook until heated through, being careful not to break up the tomatoes.

3. Transfer the spaghetti to a large shallow serving bowl. Top with the tomato mixture, sprinkle with the Parmigiano-Reggiano, gently toss, and serve immediately.

Whole Wheat Spaghetti with Broccoli Rabe, Lemon, and Ginger

all the fabulous flavors going on here make for a very delicious, healthful dish, and it's quick and easy to prepare, great for one of those nights you get home from work late. If you'd like, garnish the pasta with toasted pine nuts. De Cecco makes an excellent whole wheat spaghetti.

SERVES 4

1 pound whole wheat spaghetti
2 bunches broccoli rabe
⅓ cup Lemon Oil (page 214) or olive oil
1 large red onion, thinly sliced
½ cup golden raisins
1½ tablespoons julienne strips peeled fresh ginger
1 tablespoon finely grated lemon zest
3 garlic cloves, thinly sliced
1 teaspoon salt
¼ teaspoon crushed hot red pepper flakes
2 teaspoons balsamic vinegar

1. Cook the pasta in a large pot of boiling salted water according to the package directions, or until al dente. Drain in a colander; set the pot aside.

2. Meanwhile, cut off and discard the thick stems from the broccoli rabe. Cut the leaves crosswise into 1-inch-wide strips.

3. Heat the lemon oil in a large skillet over medium-high heat. Add the onion, and cook, stirring, for 2 minutes. Add the raisins, ginger, zest, garlic, salt, and pepper flakes and cook, stirring, for 2 minutes. Add the greens in batches. As the leaves of each batch begin to wilt, add another batch, turning constantly with tongs, and cook until all the greens are wilted and bright green, about 5 minutes. Add the vinegar and cook, stirring, for 1 minute.

4. Return the pasta to the cooking pot, add the broccoli rabe mixture, and toss to combine well. Serve immediately.

Gremolata Egg Noodles

a lovely side dish for roast chicken, pork, or fish.

SERVES 6 TO 8

One 12-ounce package wide egg noodles
¼ cup Lemon Oil (page 214) or olive oil
3 garlic cloves, thinly sliced
½ cup finely chopped fresh flat-leaf parsley
1 tablespoon finely grated lemon zest
1 tablespoon fresh lemon juice
½ teaspoon salt
½ teaspoon coarsely cracked black pepper
Freshly grated Parmigiano-Reggiano cheese
for serving

1. Cook the egg noodles in a large pot of boiling salted water according to the package directions, or until al dente. Drain in a colander, rinse with cool water, and drain again.

2. Meanwhile, heat the lemon oil in a large deep skillet over medium heat until hot but not smoking. Add the garlic and cook, stirring occasionally, until the garlic just begins to turn brown, about 3 minutes. Remove the pan from the heat and stir in the parsley, zest, lemon juice, salt, and pepper.

3. Add the noodles to the parsley mixture, return to medium heat, and cook, stirring, until heated through, about 2 minutes. Transfer to a serving bowl, sprinkle with the Parmigiano-Reggiano, and serve immediately.

Cannellini Beans with
Lemon and Parsley

These are rich and delicious and perfect with lamb, duck, and ham. Although the dish is modeled after the justly famous Tuscan white beans and sage, I think this version is even better. But if you want to use sage rather than the parsley, add 2 sprigs to the beans while they cook and stir in 2 teaspoons finely shredded fresh sage leaves after cooking. I think of the herb bundle as the lemon lover's bouquet garni—lots of zest along with the traditional sprigs of flat-leaf parsley and bay leaf.

SERVES 6 TO 8

1 pound cannellini beans, picked over and rinsed

Zest of 1 lemon, removed with a vegetable peeler, plus 1 tablespoon finely grated zest

6 sprigs fresh flat-leaf parsley, plus ¼ cup finely chopped parsley

1 imported bay leaf or ½ California bay leaf

1 red onion, thinly sliced

3 slices bacon

2 tablespoons Lemon Oil (page 214) or olive oil

2 garlic cloves, crushed with the side of a chef's knife

1 tablespoon fresh lemon juice

2 teaspoons salt

½ teaspoon freshly ground black pepper

1. Combine the beans and enough water to cover by 2 inches in a Dutch oven, bring to a boil over high heat, and boil for 1 minute. Remove the pot from the heat, cover, and let the beans stand for 1 hour. Drain and rinse the beans; return them to the pot.

2. Meanwhile, preheat the oven to 325°F.

3. Make the bouquet garni: Tie the strips of lemon zest, the parsley sprigs, and bay leaf together with kitchen string.

4. Add the onion, bacon, lemon oil, bouquet garni, garlic, and enough water to cover by 1 inch to the beans. Bring to a boil over high heat. Cover, transfer to the oven, and bake for about 15 minutes, or until the beans are softened but still retain their shape.

5. Drain the beans in a colander set over a bowl. Discard the bacon, bouquet garni, and garlic.

6. Transfer the beans to a serving dish and gently stir in the grated zest, the chopped parsley, the lemon juice, salt, and pepper. Add ½ cup to 1 cup of the cooking liquid, or enough to give the beans the desired consistency. Serve hot, at room temperature, or slightly chilled.

adding lemon flavor

GRAINS, PASTA, AND BEANS

- For an extra bit of flavor, add a squeeze of fresh lemon juice to the water when cooking rice. It helps keep the rice bright white too.

- Cook long-grain white rice with strips of lemon zest and sprigs of fresh basil. Just before serving, remove the zest and basil and stir in sliced toasted almonds.

- When you make risotto, flavor the stock with strips of lemon zest.

- Add a puree of cooked fresh spinach, mascarpone, and lots of lemon zest to risotto.

- Risotto with tiny turnips and lemon is perfectly wonderful in autumn.

- Another great risotto for the fall season is one with cooked cubed butternut squash, slivered fresh sage leaves, and lemon zest.

- In springtime, a risotto with diced crisp green apples, golden raisins, and lemon zest is just right.

- Make a lemon-flavored risotto with fresh asparagus and shrimp.

- Make a basmati rice pilaf with julienne strips of fresh ginger and lemon zest and whole cardamom pods; stir in whole natural pistachios after cooking.

- Make a rice pilaf with dried sour cherries, needle-thin strips of lemon zest and ginger, and fresh thyme leaves.

- Soft polenta is wonderful with lots of lemon zest and a generous dollop or two of mascarpone cheese stirred in at the end of cooking.

- Make your favorite polenta and stir in lemon zest, finely shredded fresh sage leaves, and grated Italian Fontina cheese.

- When you make Creamy Lemon Fettuccine (page 89), steep crumbled saffron threads in the cream with the lemon. Or try a fresh herb—basil is terrific. You might also add morel mushrooms or shrimp, or top the dish with buttery toasted bread crumbs.

- When you make your next batch of spaghetti with clam sauce, stir in a couple of teaspoons of finely grated lemon zest just before serving. A generous sprinkling of chopped fresh parsley is also important.

- Toss hot cooked perciatelli with Lemon Oil (page 214) or olive oil, lots of lemon zest, and chopped fresh herbs. Topping each serving with a poached or fried egg is terrific, and a dusting of freshly grated Parmigiano-Reggiano is absolutely necessary.

- Add lots of lemon zest and toasted anise seeds to your favorite *aglio olio* (garlic and olive oil) pasta.

- Toss hot cooked pasta with blanched asparagus tips, Lemon Oil (page 214) or olive oil, lemon juice and zest, and buttery toasted bread crumbs.

- Serve cooked hot pasta dressed very simply with Lemon Oil (page 214), grated Pecorino Romano cheese, lemon zest, and coarsely ground black pepper.

- Flavor a cold udon salad with lemon zest and shiso.

- Chop together golden raisins, drained capers, garlic, and lemon zest and use with

udon

Udon are thick white noodles made with wheat flour and saltwater. Available in many forms in Asian markets, both dried and fresh can be delicious. Refrigerate the fresh noodles until you are ready to use them, preferably for no more than 3 days. Dried udon noodles will last several months.

Lemon Oil (page 214) to dress hot freshly cooked pasta.

- Add finely grated lemon zest and minced fresh ginger to your favorite simple tomato sauce.

seafood, poultry, and *meat*

Seafood

Steamed Mussels with Lemon, Cream, and Parsley

Cultivated mussels are now widely available, and they are terrific—very easy to clean, and they have great flavor. Serve with crusty bread.

SERVES 4

½ **cup dry white wine or dry vermouth**
½ **cup crème fraîche or heavy cream**
2 **shallots, minced**
Zest of 1 lemon, removed with a vegetable peeler
1 **tablespoon unsalted butter**
2 **garlic cloves, mashed to a paste with** ½
    teaspoon salt
Pinch of freshly ground black pepper
4 **pounds mussels, scrubbed and debearded**
¼ **cup chopped fresh flat-leaf parsley**

1. Combine the wine, crème fraîche, shallots, zest, butter, garlic paste, and pepper in a large pot, bring to a boil over high heat, and boil for 2 minutes.

2. Add the mussels, cover, and cook, shaking the pan frequently, until the mussels open, about 3 minutes.

3. Remove from the heat and discard any mussels that have not opened. Stir in the parsley and serve hot, in large bowls.

Steamed Sea Bass with Ginger, Lemon, and Scallions

Steaming is a very pure way of cooking fish. It's the best way to retain the delicate flavor and texture, and you lose none of the precious juices. Bamboo steamers absorb any condensation and prevent those flavorful juices from being diluted.

SERVES 2

One 2-pound sea bass, cleaned
Zest of 2 lemons, removed with a zester
2 tablespoons julienne strips peeled fresh ginger
2 tablespoons finely shredded scallions, plus
    additional for garnish
2 tablespoons Lemon Oil (page 214) or vegetable
    oil
2 tablespoons light soy sauce
2 tablespoons Chinese rice wine, optional
2 teaspoons Asian sesame oil
1½ teaspoons fresh lemon juice
Salt and freshly ground pepper, preferably white

1. Rinse the fish and pat dry inside and out. With a sharp knife, score the fish diagonally almost to the bone 3 times on each side. Place half the zest, the ginger, and 2 tablespoons scallions in the cavity. Place the fish on a lightly oiled 9-inch heatproof plate deep enough to hold the juices of the fish.

2. Stir together the lemon oil, soy sauce, rice wine, if using, sesame oil, lemon juice, and salt and pepper to taste in a small bowl. Drizzle half of the soy mixture inside the fish and the remaining on top, rubbing it into the fish with your hands, especially into the score marks. Let the fish stand at room temperature for 30 minutes.

3. Place the plate in a 10-inch bamboo steamer basket and cover with the steamer lid. Fill a wok one-third full of water. Bring the water to a simmer and place the steamer over the water. Steam the fish over medium heat for about 10 minutes per inch (measured at the thickest part), or just until opaque throughout. Serve the fish in the basket, sprinkled with the remaining zest and scallions.

Snapper with Lemon Browned Butter and Capers

lemon and fish bring out the best in each other. You'll use every part of a lemon for this. First remove the zest. Then halve the lemon and squeeze the juice from one half. Remove the peel and pith from the remaining lemon half and chop the pulp, discarding the seeds.

SERVES 2

2 tablespoons clarified butter (see page 184)
1 shallot, minced
2 teaspoons fresh lemon juice
2 tablespoons finely chopped fresh flat-leaf
    parsley
1 tablespoon drained capers, finely chopped
1 tablespoon finely chopped lemon pulp
    (see headnote)
1 teaspoon finely grated lemon zest
Two 6 to 8-ounce red snapper fillets
Salt and freshly ground black pepper
Lemon slices for garnish

1. Preheat the oven to 350°F.

2. Heat the butter in a small saucepan or skillet over medium heat until it is a medium nutty brown color. Add the shallot and cook, stirring, until softened but not browned. Remove the skillet from the heat and stir in the lemon juice.

3. Stir together the parsley, capers, lemon pulp, and zest in a small bowl.

4. Arrange the fillets on a baking sheet and season with salt and pepper. Brush with the butter mixture and sprinkle with the parsley mixture. Bake for about 12 minutes, or just until cooked through. Serve immediately, garnished with the lemon slices.

Lemony Crab Cakes

If you can't get great crabmeat, don't make these—they are so exquisitely simple, they depend on the quality and freshness of the crab. When you pick over the crabmeat, do so gently and carefully, leaving the crab in the largest pieces possible. Serve these with the tartar sauce, Tomato Salsa with Lemon (page 201), or with your favorite crab cake accompaniment.

SERVES 4

¾ cup Lemon Mayonnaise (page 192) or
    mayonnaise
¼ cup sour cream
2 tablespoons coarse-grain Dijon mustard
1 large egg, lightly beaten
2 teaspoons finely grated lemon zest
Pinch of freshly ground black pepper
2 pounds lump crabmeat, picked over to
    remove shells and cartilage
Lemon-Tarragon Tartar Sauce (recipe follows)
Lemon wedges for serving

1. Preheat the oven to 400°F. Lightly oil a large baking sheet.

2. Whisk together the mayonnaise, sour cream, mustard, egg, zest, and pepper in a medium bowl until well combined. Gently fold in the crabmeat with a rubber spatula until just combined.

3. Gently form the crab mixture into eight 1-inch-thick cakes and transfer to the baking sheet.

4. Bake the crab cakes for 15 to 20 minutes, until golden brown. Let the crab cakes stand on the baking sheet for 5 minutes.

5. Transfer the crab cakes to serving plates and serve with the tartar sauce and lemon wedges.

Lemon-Tarragon Tartar Sauce

Whisk together 1 cup Lemon Mayonnaise
(page 192) or mayonnaise, ¼ cup sour cream,
1 minced shallot, 2 minced cornichons, 8 pitted
and chopped brine-cured green Mediterranean
olives, 2 teaspoons finely chopped fresh
tarragon, 1½ teaspoons Lemon Vinegar (page 213)
or cider vinegar, and hot red pepper sauce to taste
in a small bowl. Refrigerate, covered, for up to
2 days, until ready to serve.

I love lemon. *It's a kick. It's an intrusion. Whenever
a dish needs a little something and I'm not sure what
that little something is, I start off with a squirt of
lemon juice. When I need more punch, I use little chunks
of seeded lemon flesh. . . . You can be chewing away
and suddenly that burst of sun in your mouth makes
every other flavor shine.*

—Maggie Waldron

Poultry

Chicken with Lemon, Cumin, and Mint

this is a dish you might be served in a café in the Middle East. It's simple and flavorful and makes a quick dinner; it's also great for a picnic.

SERVES 4

Zest of 1 lemon, removed with a vegetable peeler
½ cup fresh lemon juice (about 2 large lemons)
⅓ cup Lemon Oil (page 214) or olive oil
2 tablespoons finely shredded fresh mint leaves
2 garlic cloves, minced
½ teaspoon paprika, preferably hot
½ teaspoon ground cumin
¼ teaspoon salt
¼ teaspoon freshly ground black pepper
**4 chicken wings, bony tips removed and
    discarded**
4 boneless chicken thighs, halved lengthwise
Lemon wedges for serving

1. Stir together the zest, lemon juice, lemon oil, 1 tablespoon of the mint, half the garlic, the paprika, cumin, salt, and pepper with a fork, in a large bowl. Add the chicken and turn to coat. Let stand at room temperature for 30 minutes, turning occasionally.

2. Preheat the broiler. Place the chicken on the broiler pan and broil 4 to 5 inches from the heat, turning once, for about 5 minutes on each side, or until golden brown and just cooked through.

3. Transfer the chicken to a platter, garnish with the lemon wedges, sprinkle with the remaining 1 table- spoon mint and garlic, and serve.

Clay-Pot Roasted Chicken with Chermoula and Olives

Clay-pot cooking can be traced back thousands of years, to when food was cooked in an open fire. It enables you to prepare quick, healthy meals with intense, fabulous flavor and allows food to retain its nutrients. Clay pots release their heat slowly, and during baking they gradually become dry, slowly misting the food with the water they were soaked in. Clay pots are the closest thing we have to Moroccan tagines (ceramic cooking utensils used for cooking in Morocco), and this is my version of that classic Moroccan dish, chicken tagine with preserved lemons and olives.

SERVES 4

½ Preserved Lemon (page 218)
One 3½-pound chicken, rinsed and patted dry
Salt and freshly ground black pepper
2 cinnamon sticks
8 sprigs fresh flat-leaf parsley, plus finely chopped parsley for garnish
2 imported bay leaves or 1 California bay leaf
4 garlic cloves, crushed with the side of a chef's knife
⅓ cup Chermoula (page 200)
20 cracked green Mediterranean olives
2 teaspoons arrowroot

1. Separate the pulp of the preserved lemon from the peel. Season the inside of the chicken with salt and pepper. Place the cinnamon sticks, parsley sprigs, preserved lemon pulp, bay leaves, and garlic cloves in the chicken cavity. With your fingertips, loosen the skin from the breasts. Rub most of the chermoula under the skin of the chicken breast, spreading it evenly; rub the outside of the chicken with the remaining chermoula. Season the chicken with salt and pepper. Tie the legs together and tuck the wings under. Let the chicken stand at room temperature for 30 minutes.

2. Meanwhile, soak the clay pot top and bottom in cold water to cover for at least 15 minutes; drain.

3. Cut the preserved lemon peel into long thin strips.

4. If the bottom of the clay pot is not glazed, fold a piece of parchment paper or foil to fit the bottom, so the chicken won't stick. Place the chicken in the clay pot. Scatter the olives and the preserved lemon peel around the chicken and pour 1 cup water into the pot. Cover the clay pot and place in the middle of the (cold) oven. Turn the oven temperature to 450°F and bake the chicken for 1 hour and 10 minutes.

5. Remove the pot from the oven and remove the chicken from the pot. Strain the cooking liquid into a small saucepan; reserve the olives and preserved lemon. Return the chicken to the pot, place the pot in the oven, and bake, uncovered, for 15 to 20 minutes longer to brown the skin.

6. Meanwhile, skim the fat off the cooking juices. Dissolve the arrowroot in 2 tablespoons cool water and stir into the juices. Heat the juices over medium heat, stirring, until slightly thickened. Cover and keep warm.

7. Transfer the chicken to a cutting board and let stand for 10 minutes.

8. Carve the chicken into serving pieces, and arrange on a platter. Top with the olives and preserved lemon, drizzle with some of the sauce, and sprinkle with the chopped parsley. Serve the remaining sauce at the table.

Tarragon-Lemon
Roast Chicken

Nothing satisfies more than a roast chicken, and roasted lemon wedges on the side make a perfect roast chicken even better. You could also cook 6 peeled shallots and 12 peeled garlic cloves along with the lemon wedges.

SERVES 4

4 tablespoons (½ stick) unsalted butter, at
    room temperature
2 tablespoons finely chopped fresh flat-leaf
    parsley
1 tablespoon finely grated lemon zest
2 teaspoons finely chopped fresh tarragon, plus
    8 sprigs
1¾ teaspoons salt
¼ teaspoon freshly ground black pepper, plus
    a pinch
One 3½-pound chicken, rinsed and patted dry
2 large lemons, each cut into 8 wedges
2 imported bay leaves or 1 California bay leaf
1 tablespoon sugar

1. Preheat the oven to 400°F.

2. Stir together the butter, 1 tablespoon of the parsley, the zest, the chopped tarragon, ¼ teaspoon of the salt, and the ¼ teaspoon pepper in a small bowl until well combined. With your fingertips, loosen the skin from the breast, place the butter mixture under the skin of the chicken breast, and spread evenly. Tuck the wings under the chicken. Place 4 lemon wedges, the tarragon sprigs, and the bay leaves in the chicken cavity. Place the chicken on a rack in a roasting pan. Sprinkle with ½ teaspoon salt and the pinch of pepper.

3. Toss together the remaining 12 lemon wedges, the sugar, and the remaining 1 teaspoon salt in a bowl. Place the lemons around the chicken.

4. Roast the chicken for about 1¼ hours, or until the juices of the thigh run clear when pierced with a paring knife; baste the chicken with the pan juices and turn the lemons every 10 minutes after the first 20 minutes.

5. Cover the chicken loosely with foil and let stand for 10 minutes. Carve the chicken and arrange on a platter.

6. Toss the lemons with the remaining 1 tablespoon parsley, arrange around the chicken, and serve.

Chicken Sauté with Lemon, Cream, and Herbs

good served all year round, this has a fresh clean flavor. Lemon does as much for chicken as for fish, as you'll see here. The lemon flavor comes through loud and clear, as well as highlighting all the other flavors.

SERVES 4

¼ cup all-purpose flour
Salt and freshly ground black pepper
4 skinless, boneless chicken breasts
2 tablespoons unsalted butter
½ cup heavy cream
½ cup Lemony Chicken Broth (page 44) or
    canned low-sodium chicken broth
2 shallots, minced
2 teaspoons finely grated lemon zest
2 teaspoons fresh thyme leaves
1 teaspoon minced fresh tarragon or ½ teaspoon
    dried
2 tablespoons fresh lemon juice

1. Stir the flour and ½ teaspoon each salt and pepper together on a plate. Lightly coat the chicken with the seasoned flour and shake off any excess.

2. Melt the butter in a medium skillet over medium heat. Add the chicken and cook, turning once, until just cooked through, 10 to 12 minutes. Transfer the chicken to a plate and keep warm.

3. Pour the cream and chicken broth into the skillet, increase the heat to medium-high, and scrape loose any browned bits on the bottom of the pan with a wooden spoon. Add the shallots, zest, thyme, and tarragon and cook, stirring frequently, until the cream is thickened, about 3 minutes. Stir in the lemon juice and season with salt and pepper.

4. Arrange the chicken on serving plates and spoon the sauce over it.

Chicken Under a "Brick" with Thyme Gremolata

This tastes as if it were grilled outside, and that's a great thing in the middle of winter. There's nothing difficult about the technique—you need to be careful not to tear the skin of the chicken, but even if you do, the chicken will still be quite delicious, so don't worry. I recommend an 11-inch pan because the chicken fits comfortably in it.

SERVES 4

3 garlic cloves, peeled
Salt
2 tablespoons finely chopped fresh flat-leaf
    parsley
1½ tablespoons fresh thyme leaves
½ cup plus 1 tablespoon Lemon Oil (page 214)
    or olive oil
Freshly ground black pepper
One 3-pound chicken, rinsed and patted dry
1 teaspoon finely grated lemon zest
Lemon wedges for serving

1. Mince 2 of the garlic cloves. Using the side of a chef's knife, mash them to a paste with a pinch of salt. Transfer to a small bowl, add 1 tablespoon each of the parsley, thyme, and lemon oil and a pinch of pepper, and stir together.

2. Remove and discard the wing tips from the chicken. With poultry shears or a chef's knife, split the chicken lengthwise through the breastbone and open it out. With the heel of your hand, press down firmly on the backbone and thigh and leg joints to flatten the chicken.

3. Starting at the neck, very gently slide your fingers under the skin to separate the skin from the meat. Spread the garlic-herb mixture evenly over the meat. Place the chicken on a platter, cover, and refrigerate for at least 1 hour, or overnight.

4. Heat the remaining ½ cup lemon oil in an 11- or 12-inch cast-iron skillet over medium heat. Sprinkle the chicken on both sides with ½ teaspoon each salt and pepper. Place the chicken skin side down in the pan. Place a smaller heavy skillet on top of the chicken (the pan should just fit inside the skillet). Place a brick or about 7 pounds of cans or other heat-safe weights on top and cook the chicken for 20 minutes, turning the skillet frequently.

5. Meanwhile, make the gremolata: Mince together the remaining 1 tablespoon parsley and 1½ teaspoons thyme, the zest, and the remaining garlic clove.

6. Remove the skillet and weights from the chicken. Carefully loosen the chicken from the sides and bottom of the pan with a metal spatula. If the skin is not a deep rich brown, cook the chicken for 5 minutes longer, or until the skin is dark brown. Lift the chicken (try not to tear the skin) with the spatula and carefully turn it over. Cook for 8 to 10 minutes longer, or until the juices run clear when the thigh is pierced with a paring knife. Place the chicken on a cutting board and sprinkle with the gremolata. Let stand for 5 minutes.

7. With poultry shears or a chef's knife, remove the backbone and cut the chicken into quarters. Arrange the chicken on a serving platter garnished with the lemon wedges.

lemon leaves

Lemon leaves, which are occasionally used in cooking, do not have a very strong flavor, but they do have a wonderful aroma. A small bunch of lemon leaves tied together makes an exquisitely perfumed brush for basting grilled foods.

Rosemary Grilled Chicken

In the summertime, cook this outdoors on the grill.

SERVES 4

¼ cup Lemon Oil (page 214) or olive oil
Zest of 1 lemon, removed with a vegetable peeler
1 tablespoon fresh lemon juice
1½ teaspoons minced fresh rosemary
1 teaspoon finely shredded fresh sage leaves
2 garlic cloves, thinly sliced
Salt and freshly ground black pepper to taste
One 3- to 3½-pound chicken, cut into 8 pieces
Lemon wedges for serving

1. Combine all the ingredients except chicken in a large bowl. Add the chicken and turn to coat. Marinate, covered and refrigerated, for 1 hour, turning occasionally.

2. Preheat the broiler. Place the chicken on the broiler pan and broil 4 to 5 inches from the heat, turning once, for 8 to 10 minutes on each side, or until the chicken is browned and the juices run clear when a thigh is pierced with a paring knife.

3. Transfer the chicken to a platter and serve hot, warm, or at room temperature, with the lemon wedges.

Lemon-and-Black-Pepper Fried Chicken

a cast-iron skillet is the best for fried chicken, and here you should use your largest one, preferably 11 to 12 inches in diameter. Fried chicken should be served warm, not hot—like a roast chicken, it needs to sit for a few minutes before serving. If you prefer to fry your chicken covered, it will cook in less time, 6 to 8 minutes per side.

SERVES 4 TO 6

1 cup buttermilk
⅓ cup finely chopped fresh flat-leaf parsley
2 scallions, finely chopped
1 tablespoon finely grated lemon zest
1½ teaspoons ground coriander
1 garlic clove, crushed with the side of a chef's knife
1 teaspoon salt
1 teaspoon coarsely cracked black pepper
One 3-pound chicken, cut into 8 serving pieces
About 4 cups vegetable oil, for frying
1 cup all-purpose flour
¼ cup yellow cornmeal

1. Stir together the buttermilk, parsley, scallions, zest, coriander, garlic, ¾ teaspoon of the salt, and ¾ teaspoon of the pepper in a large bowl until well combined. Add the chicken and turn to coat. Refrigerate, covered, for 3 hours, turning occasionally.

2. Let the chicken stand at room temperature for 30 minutes.

3. Meanwhile, heat the oil (it should be about ¾ inch deep) in a large skillet over medium heat until hot but not smoking. Stir together the flour, cornmeal, and the remaining ¼ teaspoon salt and ¼ teaspoon pepper on a plate.

4. Lightly coat the chicken with the seasoned flour and shake off any excess. Place the chicken on a wire rack.

5. Fry the chicken, in batches, until golden brown and cooked through, about 8 to 10 minutes per side. (If the oil begins to smoke, reduce the heat; if the oil stops bubbling around the chicken pieces, raise the heat.) Remove the chicken with tongs, drain on paper towels, and serve warm.

Meat

Classic Osso Buco with Gremolata

This classic recipe from Lombardy in Italy really highlights what lively lemon flavor can do for a dish. If you want to get seriously cross-cultural, add some Preserved Lemon peel (page 218) to the sauce or to the gremolata.

SERVES 4

4 center-cut veal shanks (each about 12 ounces and 1½ inches thick)
½ cup all-purpose flour
6 tablespoons (¾ stick) unsalted butter
3 small red onions, chopped
1 carrot, chopped
1 celery stalk with leaves, chopped
3 garlic cloves, thinly sliced
6 sprigs fresh flat-leaf parsley
Zest of 1 lemon, removed with a vegetable peeler
2 imported bay leaves or 1 California bay leaf
1 cup dry white wine
1 cup canned crushed tomatoes
1 cup chicken stock, canned low-sodium chicken broth, or water
Gremolata (page 198)
Hot cooked orzo for serving, optional

1. Pierce the skin surrounding the veal shanks with a fork so they won't curl when cooked. Tie a length of kitchen string crosswise around each one. Dredge lightly with flour, shaking off any excess.

2. Melt the butter in a Dutch oven over medium heat. Brown the veal shanks on both sides, in two batches, about 5 minutes on each side. With tongs, transfer the veal shanks to a plate. Add the onions, carrot, celery, and garlic to the pot and cook, stirring and scraping up any browned bits on the bottom, until softened, about 8 minutes.

3. Meanwhile, make a bouquet garni: Tie together the parsley sprigs, zest, and bay leaves with kitchen string.

4. Increase the heat under the pot to high, add the wine, and cook, stirring frequently, until the wine has evaporated. Add the tomatoes, stock, bouquet garni, and veal shanks, reduce the heat to low, and cook, covered, at a bare simmer for 1½ hours. Remove the lid and cook for 30 minutes longer, until the veal is very tender.

5. Stir in half of the gremolata and cook for 5 minutes longer. Remove from the heat. Remove the string from the veal shanks. Place the orzo, if using, on heated serving plates. Top with the veal shanks and sauce, and serve sprinkled with the remaining gremolata.

Wiener Schnitzel

Wiener schnitzel is a classic Austrian dish made with thin, tender veal cutlets fried in butter. Lemon forms a great alliance with capers, and you'll see that here. If your capers are large, you might want to chop them.

SERVES 6

6 veal cutlets (about 1½ pounds total; each
    ¼ inch thick)
2 large eggs
½ cup all-purpose flour
1¼ teaspoons salt
½ teaspoon freshly ground black pepper
1¼ cups dried bread crumbs
4 tablespoons (½ stick) unsalted butter
6 anchovy fillets, drained, optional
2 tablespoons drained capers
2 tablespoons finely chopped fresh flat-leaf
    parsley, for garnish
2 lemons, each cut into 6 wedges

1. Between sheets of wax paper, pound the cutlets to a ⅛-inch thickness with a meat mallet or the bottom of a small heavy saucepan.

2. Beat the eggs in a pie plate. Combine the flour, salt, and pepper on a plate. Place the bread crumbs on another plate.

3. Dredge the veal in the flour, dip into the eggs, letting the excess drain off, and then coat with the bread crumbs.

4. Melt 2 tablespoons of the butter in a large nonstick skillet over medium-high heat. Cook the veal, in two batches, until browned, 3 to 4 minutes on each side; add more butter as needed. Transfer the cutlets to a warm platter as they are browned.

5. Top the cutlets with the anchovies, if using, and the capers, and sprinkle with the parsley. Serve the lemon wedges on the side.

Sunday Pot Roast with Lemon and Root Vegetables

here's a great example of how lemon highlights other flavors. This takes a little bit of time to put together, but then all you need to do is pop it in the oven and let it cook while you relax and do Sunday things. It's a complete meal—meat and lots of vegetables. Feel free to use red wine and/or stock or broth instead of the water.

SERVES 8 TO 10

.

¼ cup Lemon Oil (page 214) or vegetable oil
One 4-pound trimmed beef brisket
3 red onions, sliced
4 slender carrots, cut into 2-inch lengths
4 slender parsnips, peeled and cut into 2-inch lengths
¼ cup all-purpose flour
8 sprigs fresh flat-leaf parsley, plus ¼ cup finely chopped parsley
Zest of 1 lemon, removed with a vegetable peeler
1 imported bay leaf or ½ California bay leaf
2 tablespoons brown sugar
4 garlic cloves, halved
1 teaspoon salt
¼ teaspoon freshly ground black pepper

1. Preheat the oven to 325°F.

2. Heat the lemon oil in a large Dutch oven over medium heat. Add the beef and brown on all sides, about 15 minutes total; transfer to a platter. Add the onions, carrots, and parsnips to the pot and cook over medium-high heat, stirring, until lightly browned on the edges, about 10 minutes. Add the flour and cook, stirring, until light brown, about 3 minutes.

3. Meanwhile, make a bouquet garni: Tie together the parsley sprigs, the zest, and bay leaf with kitchen string.

4. Add 3 cups water, the bouquet garni, brown sugar, garlic, salt, and pepper to the pot and bring to a boil. Return the beef and any accumulated juices to the pot, layering the beef between the vegetables. Cover, transfer to the oven, and cook for 2½ hours, or until the beef is very tender.

5. Remove the pot roast from the Dutch oven and transfer to a cutting board. With a slotted spoon, transfer the vegetables to a bowl, and toss with 1 tablespoon of the chopped parsley. Cover and keep warm.

6. Discard the bouquet garni and bring the sauce to a boil over high heat. Reduce the heat to medium-high and boil, stirring occasionally, for 10 minutes, or until the sauce is slightly thickened. Remove the pot from the heat and stir in 2 tablespoons of the chopped parsley.

7. To serve, slice the pot roast against the grain into ¼-inch-thick slices. Arrange the slices in the center of a serving platter, arrange the vegetables around them, and spoon some sauce over the beef. Garnish the platter with the remaining 1 tablespoon chopped parsley, and pass the remaining sauce at the table.

Leg of Lamb with Moroccan-Flavored Eggplant

Cooking the eggplant, peppers, and tomatoes with the lamb gives the vegetables a wonderful, deep flavor. Adding the Preserved Lemon peel, cilantro, coriander, and cumin gives both the vegetables and the lamb a hearty Moroccan flavor.

SERVES 8

1 medium eggplant, cut into ¾-inch pieces

2 yellow, orange, and/or red bell peppers, cored, seeded, and cut into ¼-inch-wide strips

One 28-ounce can crushed tomatoes

¼ cup plus 2 tablespoons Lemon Oil (page 214) or olive oil

Peel of ½ Preserved Lemon (page 218), cut lengthwise into ¼-inch-wide strips

4 garlic cloves, thinly sliced

1 teaspoon ground coriander

1 teaspoon ground cumin

Salt and freshly ground black pepper

One 7½-pound bone-in leg of lamb, trimmed and patted dry

¼ cup finely chopped fresh cilantro

1. Preheat the oven to 450°F.

2. Stir together the eggplant, peppers, tomatoes, ¼ cup of the lemon oil, the preserved lemon peel, garlic, coriander, cumin, and salt and pepper to taste in the center of a large deep roasting pan. Place the lamb on top, drizzle with the remaining 2 tablespoons lemon oil, and season with salt and pepper.

3. Roast the lamb for 15 minutes. Reduce the oven temperature to 350°F and roast, basting the lamb with the pan juices and stirring the vegetables every 15 minutes, for 1½ to 1¾ hours longer, until the lamb registers 150°F on an instant-read meat thermometer for medium-rare, or to the desired doneness.

4. Transfer the lamb to a cutting board and let it stand, loosely covered with foil, for 15 minutes. Transfer the eggplant mixture to a bowl, stir in the cilantro, and season with salt and pepper if necessary; cover to keep warm.

5. Carve the lamb and arrange it on a serving platter. Serve the vegetables on the side.

To Mediterranean *cooking the juice of the lemon is vital. It is the astringent corrective, as well as the flavoring, for olive-oil-based dishes and fat meat. And to me lentil soup or puree is unthinkable without the complement of lemon and olive oil; then, just try to imagine lamb kebabs without lemon. . . .*

—Elizabeth David,
An Omelette and a Glass of Wine

Pork Tenderloin with Lemon and Fennel

Simple and elegant, the combination of pork, fennel, and lemon is a natural. Grind the fennel seeds in a spice grinder, coffee grinder, or with a mortar and pestle, not to a powder, but just until coarsely ground.

SERVES 4 TO 6

3 tablespoons Lemon Oil (page 214) or olive oil
2 garlic cloves, mashed to a paste with ½ teaspoon salt
1 tablespoon finely grated lemon zest
2 teaspoons fennel seeds, coarsely ground (see headnote)
½ teaspoon freshly ground black pepper
2 pork tenderloins (1½ pounds total), trimmed

1. Combine 1 tablespoon of the lemon oil, the garlic paste, zest, fennel seeds, and pepper in a small bowl. Rub the mixture over the pork tenderloins and let stand at room temperature, covered, for 30 minutes.

2. Preheat the oven to 425°F.

3. Heat the remaining 2 tablespoons lemon oil in a large skillet over medium heat. Brown the pork tenderloins on all sides, about 5 minutes total. Transfer to a roasting pan.

4. Roast the pork for 15 to 20 minutes, or until an instant-read thermometer inserted in the thickest part of the meat registers 160°F for medium-rare, or to the desired doneness. Transfer the pork to a platter and let sit for 10 minutes before cutting into thin slices.

VARIATION:

If you'd like to serve fresh fennel alongside the pork, cut 1 fennel bulb into long thin strips. After transferring the pork to the oven, add the fennel to the skillet and cook, stirring frequently, over medium heat until it begins to brown, about 10 minutes. Add 1 garlic clove, minced, and 1 teaspoon sugar and cook, stirring, for 1 minute. Add ¾ cup water, bring to a boil, and simmer until all the liquid is evaporated and the fennel is fork-tender, about 5 minutes. Stir in 1 tablespoon fresh lemon juice and season with salt and pepper. Keep warm until ready to serve.

adding lemon flavor

SEAFOOD

- Brush fish fillets or steaks with a mixture of fresh lemon juice, zest, butter, and fresh tarragon or another favorite herb before broiling or grilling.

- Stir-fry shrimp in Lemon Oil (page 214) or olive oil with lemon zest, fresh basil leaves, and just a splash of Lemoncello (page 164).

- Make fish brochettes with lots of bay leaves and lemon slices between the chunks of fish.

- Serve your summertime lobster rolls with fresh basil leaves and Lemon Mayonnaise (page 192).

- Stir-fry shrimp in a mixture of lemon juice and zest, Chinese 5-spice powder, julienned fresh ginger, and honey.

- Marinate scallops in a lemony marinade, then thread them onto long rosemary sprigs and grill.

- Toss together a Greek-style fish salad with chopped fresh tomato, finely diced sweet red onion, and fresh oregano leaves, dressed with lemon juice.

- Stuff a whole red mullet or snapper with thin lemon and orange slices and long, thin strips of fresh fennel before roasting.

- Brush fish steaks or jumbo shrimp with lots of lemon zest and Lemon Oil (page 214) before grilling, and serve over Parsley Salad with Lemon Vinaigrette (page 58).

- Serve grilled fresh sardines with Chermoula (page 200).

- Stuff a whole fresh trout with lemon-and-almond-flavored couscous before roasting, or serve the couscous on the side.

- Serve grilled salmon with Lemon Salsa Verde (page 197).

- Serve tuna burgers with Lemon Persillade (page 197), Lemon, Mint, and Olive Relish (page 204), or Moroccan-Style Lemon, Red Onion, and Parsley Salsa (page 202).

- Make a pan sauce of equal parts sherry and sherry vinegar, flavored with lemon zest, for sautéed salmon fillets.

- Add finely grated lemon zest and ground coriander to the batter for frying fish or shellfish. Serve with lots of lemon wedges.

~ When baking whole fish, first sprinkle the fish inside and out with lemon juice, then baste with a mixture of chopped scallions, minced parsley, lemon zest, and melted butter or olive oil.

POULTRY

~ Place thin lemon slices under the skin of a chicken or turkey before roasting it, and cut a lemon into quarters and tuck them into the cavity of the bird.

~ Dredge chicken with flour seasoned with lemon zest and fresh thyme leaves before frying.

~ Roast a chicken with sliced sweet potatoes and lemon wedges on the side.

~ Served sliced poached chicken with Avgolemono Sauce (page 190).

~ Add lemon zest and poppy seeds to chicken paprikash.

~ Brush quail with a mixture of fresh lemon juice and molasses before grilling or roasting.

MEAT

~ Add pieces of Oven-Dried Lemon Zest (page 15) to braises and stews.

~ Add fresh lemon juice to any lamb dish— the flavor combination is a natural.

~ Add a large pinch of lemon zest to your favorite meat loaf or meatball recipe.

~ Serve grilled filet mignon, or any other cut of steak, with Lemon Salsa Verde (page 197).

~ Chopped Preserved Lemon peel (page 218) and pitted green Mediterranean olives make a fabulous stuffing for a boneless pork loin roast.

~ Add julienne strips of both Preserved Lemon peel (page 218) and dried peaches to your next pot roast.

~ Flavor lamb stew with lemon juice and zest, fresh oregano, and a cinnamon stick—and, just before serving, top it with a sprinkling of crumbled feta cheese.

desserts

Lemon Pound Cake

this is a perfect tea cake, a perfect dessert, even the perfect breakfast. In fact, it's just right for every occasion and nonoccasion. Having one at the ready in the freezer is never a bad idea.

SERVES 10

1⅔ cups all-purpose flour
2 teaspoons baking powder
¼ teaspoon salt
1 cup sugar
8 tablespoons (1 stick) unsalted butter, at room temperature
2 large eggs
½ cup milk
2 tablespoons finely grated lemon zest
¼ cup fresh lemon juice

1. Position a rack in the center of the oven. Preheat the oven to 350°F. Butter and flour a 4 X 8-inch loaf pan.

2. Sift the flour, baking powder, and salt together twice.

3. With an electric mixer on medium-high speed, beat ¾ cup of the sugar and the butter in a large bowl until light and fluffy, about 2 minutes. Beat in the eggs one at a time, beating well after each addition. Beat in the milk and zest. Add the flour mixture and beat on low speed just until combined, scraping down the sides of the bowl once or twice. Transfer the batter to the prepared pan and smooth the top with a rubber spatula.

4. Bake for 50 to 55 minutes, until a wooden toothpick inserted in the center comes out clean. Cool the cake in the pan on a wire rack for 10 minutes, then turn it out onto the rack.

5. Meanwhile, heat the remaining ¼ cup sugar and the lemon juice in a small saucepan over medium heat, stirring until the sugar is dissolved.

6. Poke 1-inch-deep holes all over the top of the cake with a toothpick. Brush the top of the hot cake with the hot glaze; if the glaze does not sink into the cake, poke more holes in the top. Let the cake cool completely before serving.

The way you measure the flour for a recipe is crucial to the final outcome. For these recipes, stir the flour in the canister to aerate it, then spoon it into the measuring cup and level the top with a table knife. Dipping the measuring cup into the flour will give you a different amount of flour.

Lemon Galette

Although it is made with a sweet yeast dough, this is a very simple (and very elegant) French-style dessert. *Galette* is French for a type of cake, but this is more like a sweet pizza, and it is charming served with sliced ripe strawberries or sliced summer fruits. The coriander adds an aromatic lemony flavor.

SERVES 6 TO 8

One ¼-ounce package active dry yeast
4 tablespoons (½ stick) unsalted butter, at
    room temperature
2 tablespoons light brown sugar
1 large egg
2 tablespoons finely grated lemon zest
¾ teaspoon ground coriander
½ teaspoon salt
1⅔ cups all-purpose flour
½ cup crème fraîche or sour cream
2 tablespoons granulated sugar

1. Sprinkle the yeast over 6 tablespoons warm water (110° to 115°F) in a large bowl. Let stand for 10 minutes.

2. Add the butter, brown sugar, egg, zest, coriander, and salt and beat with an electric mixer on medium speed for a minute or two; the mixture will look curdled. Add the flour in 3 batches, beating on low speed and scraping down the sides of the bowl as necessary, just until well combined.

3. Turn the dough out onto a lightly floured surface and knead until smooth, about 3 minutes. Place the dough in a lightly floured bowl, cover with a towel, and let rise in a warm place until doubled in size, about 1½ hours.

4. Gently punch down the dough. Transfer it to a lightly floured surface and knead lightly. Roll out the dough to a 13-inch circle and place it on an oiled 12-inch pizza pan or large baking sheet. Fold over a 1-inch rim all around the edge of the dough. Spread the crème fraîche evenly over the dough and sprinkle with the granulated sugar. Let rise for 20 minutes.

5. Preheat the oven to 500°F.

6. Bake the galette for 6 to 8 minutes, until golden brown. Serve warm, cut into wedges with a pizza wheel or kitchen scissors.

Lemon Meringue Pie

don't you love the way the tender cloud of meringue contrasts with the tart, creamy golden yellow filling? Remember that the meringue will shrink unless you spread it all the way to the crust to form a seal. You won't find any cornstarch in this version, which makes for a richer filling that's not quite as firm.

SERVES 8

PASTRY CRUST

1⅓ cups all-purpose flour

2 teaspoons sugar

½ teaspoon salt

6 tablespoons (¾ stick) chilled unsalted butter, cut into small pieces

FILLING

1½ cups sugar

1 tablespoon finely grated lemon zest

¼ teaspoon salt

3 large eggs

4 large egg yolks

¾ cup fresh lemon juice (about 3 large lemons)

8 tablespoons (1 stick) unsalted butter, cut into 8 pieces, at room temperature

MERINGUE

4 large egg whites

Pinch of salt

¼ cup plus 2 tablespoons sugar

½ teaspoon pure vanilla extract

1. Make the pastry crust: Stir together the flour, sugar, and salt in a medium bowl. Cut in the butter with a pastry blender or two knives, used scissors-fashion, until the mixture forms coarse crumbs. Pour ¼ cup ice-cold water into a glass measure. Sprinkle 1 tablespoon of the water over the flour mixture, stirring gently with a fork to moisten it evenly. Continue adding water, 1 tablespoon at a time, just until the dough begins to hold together when a small bit is pressed between your fingers; you may not need to use all of the water. Press the dough together to form a ball and knead lightly. Shape it into a disk, wrap in wax paper, and refrigerate for at least 30 minutes, and up to 2 days.

2. Position a rack in the middle of the oven and preheat the oven to 425°F.

3. Roll out the dough on a lightly floured surface to a 12-inch round. Transfer the dough to a 9-inch glass pie plate and gently press it against the bottom and sides. Trim the dough, leaving a ¾-inch overhang, turn it under, and crimp as desired. Prick the bottom and sides of the dough all over with a fork. Line the pastry shell with heavy-duty aluminum foil and fill with uncooked beans or rice.

4. Bake the pastry shell for 12 minutes. Remove the foil and beans and bake for 8 minutes longer, or until light golden brown. Let cool on a wire rack. Reduce the oven temperature to 350°F.

5. Make the filling: Process the sugar, zest, and salt in a food processor until the zest is finely ground. Transfer to a large heavy saucepan, add the eggs, egg yolks, and lemon juice, and whisk until smooth. Add 4 tablespoons of the butter and cook, whisking constantly, over medium-low heat, stirring until the filling is very thick and the whisk leaves a definite trail, about 12 minutes. Whisk in the remaining 4 tablespoons butter. Remove the pan from the heat and let cool for 5 minutes, whisking occasionally, then pour into the cooled crust.

6. Make the meringue: Beat the egg whites in a large bowl with an electric mixer on medium speed just until foamy. Increase the speed to medium-high, add the salt, and beat just to soft peaks. Add the sugar, 1 tablespoon at a time, and beat just to stiff peaks. Add the vanilla and beat to combine well.

7. Top the filling with the meringue mixture, using a rubber spatula to create a smooth, domed top and making certain that the meringue touches the crust all around to seal in the filling. If desired, form swirls in the meringue, using a small spoon, starting in the center of the meringue.

8. Bake for 10 to 12 minutes, or until the meringue is golden brown. Let cool to room temperature on a wire rack.

Shaker Lemon Pie

After a long *period abroad nothing could make me more homesick than an American magazine ad of a luscious layer cake, except one, and that was a pictured lemon pie.*

—Irma Rombauer, *Joy of Cooking* (1943)

a classic—very simple, very lemony, and very refreshing. A specialty of the Shaker sisters in Ohio, dating back to the early 1800s, this can be a bit surprising for those who have never had the experience of a Shaker lemon pie, made with sliced lemons, peel and all. This recipe is adapted from one in *The Shaker Cook Book,* by Caroline B. Piercy.

Use your sharpest knife. The lemon slices don't have to be perfect, but they do need to be very thin. Consider serving this with rich vanilla ice cream.

SERVES 8

4 small thin-skinned lemons
2 cups plus 1 tablespoon sugar
2¼ cups all-purpose flour
½ teaspoon salt
⅔ cup cold vegetable shortening
4 large eggs, lightly beaten
1 tablespoon milk

1. Slice off the tops and bottoms of the lemons, then cut 2 of the lemons lengthwise in half, then crosswise into paper-thin slices, and discard the seeds. With the remaining 2 lemons, following the natural curve of the fruit, carefully cut down from the top to the bottom with a small sharp knife, removing the peel and pith in thick strips. Cut the peeled lemons into thin slices and discard the seeds.

2. Transfer the lemon slices and any accumulated juices to a bowl and stir in 2 cups of the sugar. Let stand, covered, at room temperature, for at least 4 hours, or, preferably, overnight.

3. Stir together the flour and salt in a medium bowl. Cut in the shortening with a pastry blender or 2 knives, used scissors-fashion, until the pieces of shortening are the size of small peas. Place ⅓ cup ice-cold water in a glass measure. Sprinkle 1 tablespoon of the water over the flour mixture, stirring gently with a fork to moisten it evenly. Continue adding water, 1 tablespoon at a time, just until the dough begins to hold together when a small bit is pressed between your fingers; you may not need to use all of the water. Press the dough together to form a ball and knead lightly. Divide the dough into 2 pieces, one slightly larger than the other. Shape into 2 disks, wrap in wax paper, and refrigerate for at least 30 minutes, and up to 2 days.

4. On a lightly floured surface, roll out the larger piece of the dough to a 12-inch round. Fit the dough into a 9-inch glass pie plate. Trim the edge of the dough, leaving a ½-inch overhang, and fold the excess dough under itself. Refrigerate for 30 minutes.

5. Position a rack in the lower third of the oven and preheat the oven to 450°F.

6. On the lightly floured surface, roll out the remaining dough to a 10-inch round. Stir the eggs into the lemon mixture until thoroughly combined. Spoon into the pie crust. Cover with the dough and trim and crimp the edges. Brush the crust with the milk. Cut 4 steam vents into the top of the crust using a small sharp knife and sprinkle with the remaining 1 tablespoon sugar.

7. Bake the pie for 20 minutes. Reduce the heat to 350°F and bake for 25 to 30 minutes more, until the crust is golden and a thin knife inserted into one of the slashes comes out fairly clean. Let the pie cool to room temperature on a wire rack before serving.

Lemon Tart with Brown Butter Crust

You can use regular melted butter for the crust, but the brown butter adds a wonderful richness.

SERVES 8

¼ cup plus 2 tablespoons clarified unsalted
    butter (see page 184)
1½ cups all-purpose flour
2 tablespoons sugar
Pinch of salt
½ cup heavy cream
Lemon Curd (page 228), chilled

1. Position a rack in the middle of the oven and preheat the oven to 350°F.

2. Heat the butter in a small saucepan or skillet over medium-high heat until it is a nutty brown color. Immediately pour the butter into a glass measure and let cool to room temperature.

3. Stir together the flour, sugar, and salt in a medium bowl. Pour in the butter in a fine stream, stirring constantly with a fork, and continue stirring until the dough begins to hold together when a small bit is pressed between your fingers.

4. Transfer the dough to a 9-inch fluted tart pan with a removable bottom. Press the dough evenly into the bottom and up the sides of the pan. Trim the edges of dough, and prick the bottom and side of the dough all over with a fork. Bake for 20 minutes, or until the crust is light golden brown. Let cool to room temperature on a wire rack.

5. With an electric mixer on medium-high speed, beat the cream in a medium bowl just to soft peaks. Whisk in the lemon curd just until blended.

6. Pour the filling into the crust. Refrigerate for at least 3 hours, or until thoroughly chilled.

Jane Grigson's Lemon Honeycomb Mould

this recipe is adapted from Jane Grigson, one of my favorite food writers. She was erudite, witty, and practical, and I always feel I can trust her. She knew a great deal and never lost sight of the fact that it's really just dinner and not too, too serious. It's her recommendation to put this custard into an elaborately patterned mold, and she cautions against using low-fat or fat-free milk. Her description of the dessert: "It will have a cap of clear lemon jelly, then a thin band of opaque cream jelly shading off into a honeycombed spongy base which makes a slight crinkling noise as it's eaten."

SERVES 6

3 large eggs, separated
1 tablespoon finely grated lemon zest
½ cup heavy cream
⅓ cup sugar
Two ¼-ounce envelopes gelatin
1½ cups whole milk
¼ cup plus 2 tablespoons fresh lemon juice

1. Whisk together the egg yolks, zest, cream, sugar, and gelatin in a heatproof bowl.

2. Heat the milk in a saucepan over medium-high heat to just below boiling. Whisking constantly, add the milk in a thin stream to the yolk mixture.

3. Fill a large saucepan with about 1½ inches of water and bring the water to a simmer. Place the bowl over the simmering water and stir with a wooden spoon until the custard thickens and leaves a path on the back of the spoon when you draw your finger across it. Add the lemon juice and pour the mixture through a strainer into a large glass measure or a bowl.

4. With an electric mixer on high speed, beat the egg whites in a large bowl just to stiff peaks. Fold in the hot custard with a whisk. Let stand for about 5 minutes. Pour the mixture into a 1-quart mold. Chill for about 4 hours, or until firmly set.

5. To serve, slide a knife around the edge of the pudding, and turn it out onto a plate (if your decorative mold makes it impossible to use a knife, dip the mold into hot water for about 5 seconds, then invert the dessert onto the plate).

quick chill

If you don't want to wait for a frozen dessert mixture to chill before freezing, do a "quick chill": put the mixture in a large glass measure or a deep bowl and place it in a shorter bowl. Add ice and water to the bowl and stir or whisk occasionally, adding fresh ice and water as the ice melts, until the mixture is chilled. (Make sure that no ice water gets into the mixture you're cooling.) This also works well for chilling soups or broth, sauces, lemonade, or other drink mixtures.

Lemon-Caramel Ice Cream

Caramel is easy to make. Use the heaviest saucepan you've got, and brush down the sides of the pan with a wet pastry brush so the sugar won't crystallize. Don't be tempted to pull the caramel off the heat when it's only light golden brown— let it get dark for better flavor, and be ready to pour in the cream to stop the cooking. But be careful, it will spatter.

MAKES I QUART

2 cups heavy cream
2 tablespoons finely grated lemon zest
¾ cup sugar
1¼ cups milk
6 large egg yolks
½ teaspoon salt
¼ cup fresh lemon juice
1 teaspoon pure vanilla extract

1. Bring the cream to a boil in a medium saucepan over medium-high heat. Remove the pan from the heat, add the zest, and let stand, covered, while you make the caramel.

2. Combine the sugar and 2 tablespoons water in a large heavy saucepan and heat over medium-low heat, stirring, until the sugar is dissolved. Increase the heat to high and boil, without stirring but occasionally brushing down the sides of the pan with a wet pastry brush and swirling the pan, until the caramel is a dark amber color.

3. Immediately remove the pan from the heat and carefully stir in the cream mixture, using a long-handled wooden spoon, until well combined. Stir in the milk.

4. Whisk together the egg yolks and salt in a medium bowl until smooth. Whisk ½ cup of the hot caramel mixture into the yolks, then gradually whisk in the remaining caramel mixture, ½ cup at a time. Return the mixture to the saucepan. Cook the custard over low heat, stirring constantly with a wooden spoon, until it thickens and leaves a path on the back of the spoon when you draw your finger across it; do not let the custard simmer, or it will curdle. Immediately pour the custard through a strainer into a bowl.

5. Let the custard cool to room temperature. Refrigerate, tightly covered, for at least 4 hours, until completely chilled, or overnight. Or "quick-chill" the custard (see page 140).

6. Pour the lemon juice through a strainer into the custard, and whisk in the vanilla. Freeze the custard in an ice cream machine according to the manufacturer's instructions. Transfer to a freezer container and store in the freezer until ready to serve.

Lemon-Fennel Sorbet

The fennel seeds in this sorbet give it a touch of extra sweetness and a dimension that's a little mysterious—not everyone can guess what it is. But you don't have to use them. You can make a fantastic lemon sorbet without them. Or consider flavoring the sorbet with lemongrass, rosemary, or kaffir lime leaves.

MAKES 1 QUART

1½ cups sugar
Zest of 1 lemon, removed with a vegetable peeler
1 teaspoon fennel seeds
1½ cups fresh lemon juice (about 6 large
lemons)
¼ teaspoon salt

1. Combine 1½ cups water and the sugar in a medium saucepan and bring just to a boil over medium-high heat, stirring until the sugar is dissolved. Remove the pan from the heat, add the zest and fennel seeds, and let stand, covered, for 10 minutes.

2. Pour the sugar syrup through a strainer into a medium bowl. Stir in the lemon juice and salt and let cool to room temperature. Refrigerate, covered, for about 3 hours, until thoroughly chilled; or "quick-chill" the mixture (see page 140).

3. Transfer the mixture to an ice cream maker and freeze according to the manufacturer's instructions. After churning, the sorbet will be soft but ready to eat. For a firmer texture, transfer to a freezer container and freeze for at least 2 hours before serving.

Lemonade Granita

Use any of the flavor variations of Old-fashioned Lemonade. Don't scoop this dessert; serve it by raking along the top with a fork to give a fluffiness to the crystals.

SERVES 6

Old-fashioned Lemonade (page 151), or any of the variations, at room temperature

1. Place a 9 X 13-inch baking pan in the freezer until very cold.

2. Pour the lemonade mixture through a strainer into the cold baking pan. Cover the pan with aluminum foil and freeze the mixture for 1 hour, or until ice crystals form around the edge.

3. Stir the mixture well with a fork to incorporate the ice and break up any chunks. Continue to freeze, stirring every 30 minutes, for 2 hours, or until the granita has become granular but is still slightly slushy.

4. Serve the granita, or freeze for up to 4 hours, stirring once or twice to break up any large chunks of ice.

Ginger Lemon Bars

If you're not a ginger lover, just leave it out. You'll still have a luscious, tart and tangy, sweet lemon bar.

MAKES 16 BARS

1 cup plus 2 tablespoons all-purpose flour
1¾ cups confectioners' sugar, plus additional
for dusting
½ teaspoon ground ginger
Pinch of salt
8 tablespoons (1 stick) chilled unsalted butter,
cut into small pieces
½ teaspoon baking powder
3 large eggs
¼ cup plus 2 tablespoons fresh lemon juice

1. Position a rack in the middle of the oven and preheat the oven to 350°F. Butter an 8-inch square baking pan.

2. Stir together 1 cup of the flour, ¼ cup of the sugar, the ginger, and salt in a medium bowl. Cut in the butter with a pastry blender or 2 knives, used scissors-fashion, until the mixture forms coarse crumbs. Knead the dough in the bowl just until it begins to come together.

3. Transfer the dough to the baking pan and press it evenly over the bottom. Bake for 25 minutes, or until light golden brown. Let cool on a wire rack while you make the filling.

4. Stir together the remaining 1½ cups sugar, the remaining 2 tablespoons flour, and the baking powder in a small bowl.

5. With an electric mixer on high speed, beat the eggs in a medium bowl until pale yellow and tripled in volume, about 2 minutes. Reduce the speed to low, add the sugar mixture, and beat just until blended, scraping down the sides of the bowl as needed. Add the lemon juice and beat just until blended.

6. Pour the lemon mixture over the warm crust. Bake for 18 to 20 minutes, until the filling is just set in the center. Let cool to room temperature on a wire rack.

7. Just before serving, sift confectioners' sugar lightly over the cookies. Cut into 2-inch squares. Store in an airtight container.

Lemon Sablés

Sablé means "sandy" in French, and these cookies have a very pleasant slightly gritty texture. They may be rich and buttery classic French cookies, but they are very easy to prepare. Because the dough can get very soft and sticky, you might want to place it in the refrigerator for a few minutes before rolling it into a log.

MAKES ABOUT 28 COOKIES

¾ cup sugar

2 tablespoons finely grated lemon zest

½ pound (2 sticks) unsalted butter, at room temperature

½ teaspoon pure Lemon Oil (see page 214), optional

1 large egg

1 teaspoon pure vanilla extract

2 cups all-purpose flour

¼ teaspoon salt

1. Pulse the sugar and lemon zest in a food processor until finely ground.

2. With an electric mixer on medium-low speed, beat the butter, the sugar mixture, and the lemon oil, if using, in a large bowl until light and creamy, about 2 minutes. Add the egg and vanilla and beat until well combined. Sift in the flour and salt and beat with a wooden spoon just until incorporated.

3. Divide the dough in half. Form each half into a 7-inch log on a sheet of wax paper. Tightly wrap in the paper and refrigerate for at least 2 hours. The dough can be refrigerated for up to 1 week; for longer storage, place in a self-sealing plastic bag and freeze for up to 1 month.

4. Position a rack in the middle of the oven and preheat the oven to 325°F. Line a large baking sheet with parchment paper.

5. Slice 1 log of dough into ⅜-inch-thick rounds and place them about 2 inches apart on the baking sheet. Bake for 17 minutes, or until the edges of the cookies are a pale golden brown. Transfer the cookies to a wire rack to cool. Repeat with the remaining log. Store the cookies in a tightly covered container for up to 3 days.

Peaches and Berries with Lemon and Rose Water

This recipe calls for mixed berries, but you can use one type, too. Blueberries are best. But ripe black-berries and raspberries are awfully good, too. If you use strawberries, slice them. This is very pretty served as is, and is gorgeous garnished with (un-sprayed) rose petals or lemon blossoms. It's also delightful served with Lemon Sablés (page 146).

SERVES 4

⅓ cup sugar
4 strips lemon zest, removed with a vegetable peeler
1 tablespoon fresh lemon juice
Pinch of salt
4 ripe but firm peaches, peeled and sliced
1 to 2 teaspoons rose water (or orange flower water)
¼ teaspoon pure vanilla extract
1 cup mixed berries

1. Combine 1 cup water, the sugar, zest, lemon juice, and salt in a small saucepan and bring to a boil over high heat. Remove the pan from the heat and let cool for 2 minutes. Add the peaches and let stand for 10 minutes.

2. Add the rose water and vanilla to the mixture and let cool to room temperature.

3. Stir in the berries. Chill, covered, for at least 1 hour, and up to 4 hours, before serving.

adding lemon flavor

DESSERTS

- Serve homemade or store-bought sorbet or other frozen desserts in frozen lemon shells (see page 21).

- Add lemon zest to your favorite recipes for sugar, butter, or oatmeal cookies.

- Add lemon zest to fruit compotes and dessert sauces.

- Add wide strips of lemon zest, removed with a vegetable peeler, to any poaching liquid for fruit.

- Blend fresh lemon juice and zest with sour cream or yogurt—and maybe a small amount of brown sugar and chopped candied ginger—for a great dip for sliced fresh fruit.

- Sprinkle a fresh grapefruit half with a few drops of Lemoncello (page 164) and warm it in the oven just until heated through.

- Blend grated lemon zest and lemon juice with softened frozen vanilla yogurt or ice cream.

- Bring out the flavor of ripe tropical fruits by sprinkling them with lemon juice and a pinch of sugar before serving.

- Add a squeeze of fresh juice and pinch of zest to any fruit pie or cobbler to enhance the flavor of the fruit and make it taste brighter.

lemonade and *other drinks*

Old-fashioned Lemonade

There's nothing like good old-fashioned lemonade. When you don't have the time for hours of sitting on the porch and relaxing, ten minutes with your feet up and a tall glass of lemonade will be almost as good. This is delicious with fresh fruit and/or berries added—raspberries, blueberries, sliced strawberries, apricots, nectarines, plums, and peaches are all great. If you're not using the sliced lemon or the zest, there's no need to steep the mixture for 10 minutes, but the slices or the zest sure does make the lemonade taste better.

I prefer my lemonade made with simple syrup, so there's no gritty sugar in it. I also like my lemonade strong. I don't want it to taste diluted with the first sip. If you find you don't like yours as strong, just add more water. Use the "quick-chill" method (see page 140) for this if you like.

MAKES ABOUT 5 CUPS

1 cup sugar
Pinch of salt
1 lemon, thinly sliced, or zest of 1 lemon,
     removed with a vegetable peeler
1 cup fresh lemon juice (about 4 large lemons)

1. Bring 3½ cups water, the sugar, and salt to a boil in a large saucepan over high heat, stirring until the sugar is dissolved. Remove the saucepan from the heat, add the sliced lemon, and let stand, covered, for 10 minutes.

2. Pour the sugar syrup into a pitcher, straining it, if desired. Stir in the lemon juice. Chill; serve over ice.

VARIATIONS:

Mango Lemonade
Reduce the water to 2½ cups and add 1 cup mango nectar with the lemon juice. (Or do the same with peach, apricot, guava, guanabana, passion fruit, or the nectar of your choice.)

Mint Lemonade
I love lemonade with spearmint, but any mint will do. Steep 6 large sprigs of fresh mint in the syrup with the sliced lemons; discard the mint before serving, and garnish with fresh sprigs.

Ginger Lemonade
Steep 8 slices fresh ginger (each about the size of a quarter) in the syrup with the sliced lemons; discard the ginger before serving. For **Ginger-Pear Lemonade,** use the ginger, reduce the water to 2½ cups, and add 1 cup pear nectar with the lemon juice.

kaffir lime leaves

Sometimes called "wild limes," kaffir limes are found in Southeast Asia, where their leaves are used extensively in cooking. Exceptionally aromatic, they have a pronounced clean, green perfume and flavor. The glossy oval leaves are used in the same way we use bay leaves, adding a unique and sharp citrus taste, fragrance, and zing. You can find them fresh in many Asian supermarkets; freeze them in self-sealing plastic bags.

Pear–Bay Leaf Lemonade

Steep 6 imported or 3 California bay leaves in the syrup made with 2½ cups water and sliced lemons; discard them before serving. Add 1 cup pear nectar with the lemon juice.

Kaffir Lime Leaf Lemonade

Steep 12 torn kaffir lime leaves in the syrup, with the sliced lemons; discard them before serving. Garnish the lemonade with more lime leaves, if desired.

**Orange Flower Water or
Rose Water Lemonade**

Add 1 tablespoon orange flower water or rose water with the lemon juice. Berries are especially nice in this.

Cherry-Thyme Lemonade

Steep 1 cup halved ripe cherries (with their pits) and 6 fresh thyme sprigs in the syrup with the sliced lemon; strain before serving. You might garnish with cherries on the stem and thyme sprigs.

Lavender Lemonade

Steep either ¼ cup fresh (unsprayed) lavender flowers or 1 tablespoon dried flowers in the syrup with the sliced lemon; strain before serving. Garnish with lavender stalks, if available.

Lemongrass Lemonade

Steep 2 (or more) chopped stalks of lemongrass in the syrup with the sliced lemon and strain before serving. Use trimmed lemongrass stalks as swizzle sticks, if desired. A scoop of lemon sorbet is extraordinary in this—and then it can be dessert.

Dried-Lemon Lemonade

Steep 1 or 2 whole dried lemons (see page 232) in the syrup with the sliced lemons; discard before serving.

Saffron Lemonade

Steep a pinch of crumbled saffron threads in the syrup with the sliced lemon (no need to remove before serving).

Cardamom Lemonade

Steep 6 crushed cardamom pods with the sliced lemon (no need to discard them before serving).

Frozen Lemonade

Combine Old-fashioned Lemonade and lots of ice cubes in a blender and blend until slushy.

Sorbet Lemonade

Add a scoop of sorbet to each glass of lemonade. Lemon sorbet, of course, is the best, but raspberry and mango are good too.

Yellow Jacket

Add a shot of Lemon Tequila (page 166) or tequila to each glass of lemonade; or add Lemon Vodka, Gin, or Brandy (page 166).

Lynchburg Lemonade

Add Lemon Bourbon (page 166) or bourbon, using an ounce or so per glass, to lemonade.

Liqueur Lemonade

Many liqueurs are terrific in lemonade. My favorites are Lemoncello (page 164), crème de cassis, and ginger.

Campari Lemonade

Make pink lemonade for grown-ups by adding Campari to lemonade.

Lemonade Popsicles

Freeze your favorite lemonade in Popsicle molds or small paper cups, using plastic spoons for handles.

Watermelon Lemonade

this is a beautiful pink lemonade. There's no need to seed the watermelon, but don't blend it any longer than you have to, then strain the seeds out.

MAKES ABOUT 6 CUPS

1 cup sugar
Pinch of salt
1 lemon, thinly sliced, or zest of 1 lemon, removed with a vegetable peeler
2 cups chopped watermelon
1 cup fresh lemon juice (about 4 large lemons)

1. Bring 3 cups water, the sugar, and salt to a boil in a large saucepan over high heat, stirring until the sugar is dissolved. Remove the saucepan from the heat, add the sliced lemon, and let stand, covered, for 10 minutes.

2. Meanwhile, puree the watermelon in a blender or food processor with ½ cup water.

3. Pour the syrup and the watermelon puree through a strainer into a pitcher. Stir in the lemon juice. Chill; serve over ice.

Strawberry-Rhubarb Lemonade

love strawberry-rhubarb pie? This takes a lot less time to make.

MAKES ABOUT 5 CUPS

½ pound rhubarb, trimmed and cut into 1-inch pieces
¾ cup sugar
2 strips lemon zest, removed with a vegetable peeler
½ teaspoon pure vanilla extract
Pinch of salt
2 cups sliced ripe strawberries
1 cup fresh lemon juice (about 4 large lemons)

1. Bring 3½ cups water, the rhubarb, sugar, zest, vanilla, and salt to a boil in a large saucepan over high heat, stirring until the sugar is dissolved. Reduce the heat and simmer, covered, for 8 minutes.

2. Stir in 1 cup of the strawberries and simmer, covered, for 2 minutes longer. Remove the saucepan from the heat and let stand, covered, for 5 minutes.

3. Pour the syrup through a strainer into a pitcher. Let cool, then stir in the remaining 1 cup strawberries and the lemon juice. Chill; serve over ice.

Nectarine-Basil Lemonade

an all-time favorite combination of mine is basil and nectarines—they're quintessential summer flavors. Ripe peaches could be almost as good, but you need to peel them.

MAKES ABOUT 6 CUPS

1 cup fresh basil leaves, plus additional for garnish
2 ripe but firm nectarines, 1 pitted and finely chopped, 1 pitted and thinly sliced
¾ cup sugar
Pinch of salt
1 cup fresh lemon juice (about 4 large lemons)

1. Bring 3½ cups water, the basil leaves, the chopped nectarine, sugar, and salt to a boil in a large saucepan over high heat, stirring until the sugar is dissolved. Reduce the heat and simmer, covered, for 5 minutes. Let cool to room temperature.

2. Pour the mixture through a strainer into a pitcher. Stir in the sliced nectarine and the lemon juice. Chill; serve over ice, garnished with basil leaves.

A drop in the price of West Indian sugar inspired the invention, in Paris in 1630, of lemonade. Owners of the sidewalk cafés of Paris became known as limonadiers. They sold coffee and other drinks, as they do today, but for about two centuries they were known both popularly and officially as limonadiers.
—John McPhee, *Oranges*

When life gives you lemons, make lemonade!
—Anonymous optimist

Any, Every, or Many Berry Lemonade

MAKES ABOUT 5 CUPS

1 cup sugar
Pinch of salt
1 lemon, thinly sliced, or zest of 1 lemon, removed with a vegetable peeler
1 cup ripe raspberries, blackberries, blueberries, loganberries, marionberries, and/or boysenberries, plus additional berries for garnish
1 cup fresh lemon juice (about 4 large lemons)

1. Bring 3 cups water, the sugar, and salt to a boil in a large saucepan over high heat, stirring until the sugar is dissolved. Remove the saucepan from the heat, add the sliced lemon, and let stand, covered, for 10 minutes.

2. Meanwhile, puree the berries with ½ cup water in a blender or food processor.

3. Add the berry puree to the syrup and pour through a strainer into a pitcher. Stir in the lemon juice. Chill; serve over ice, garnished with whole berries.

Coriander-Cumin-Fennel Lemonade

This may sound strange, but only until you taste it. It's really refreshing: sweet, tart, and salty.

MAKES ABOUT 5 CUPS

1 cup sugar
1 teaspoon coriander seeds
1 teaspoon cumin seeds
1 teaspoon fennel seeds
¼ teaspoon salt
¼ teaspoon black peppercorns
1 lemon, thinly sliced, or zest of 1 lemon, removed with a vegetable peeler
1 cup fresh lemon juice (about 4 large lemons)

1. Bring 3½ cups water, the sugar, coriander, cumin, fennel, salt, and peppercorns to a boil in a large saucepan over high heat, stirring until the sugar is dissolved. Cover and boil for 5 minutes. Remove the saucepan from the heat, add the sliced lemon, and let stand, covered, for 5 minutes. Let cool to room temperature.

2. Pour the syrup through a strainer into a pitcher. Stir in the lemon juice. Chill; serve over ice.

Lemon Verbena Lemonade with Strawberries

Instead of the lemon verbena, use 10 fresh scented geranium leaves (unsprayed) or a sprig of fresh rosemary.

MAKES ABOUT 5 CUPS

1 cup sugar
Pinch of salt
1 pint ripe strawberries, hulled and sliced
1 lemon, thinly sliced, or zest of 1 lemon—
   removed with a vegetable peeler
½ cup packed fresh lemon verbena leaves
   (unsprayed)
1 cup fresh lemon juice (about 4 large
   lemons)

1. Bring 3 cups water, the sugar, and salt to a boil in a large saucepan over high heat, stirring until the sugar is dissolved. Remove the saucepan from the heat and stir in 4 of the sliced strawberries, the sliced lemon, and the lemon verbena. Let stand, covered, for 10 minutes.

2. Pour the syrup through a strainer into a pitcher. Stir in the lemon juice and strawberries. Chill; serve over ice.

Tarragon-Honeydew Lemonade

This is tremendously cooling, but don't make it way ahead; it doesn't keep well.

MAKES ABOUT 5 CUPS

1 cup sugar
Pinch of salt
2 small sprigs fresh tarragon, plus additional
   sprigs for garnish
1 lemon, thinly sliced, or zest of 1 lemon,
   removed with a vegetable peeler
2 cups chopped honeydew melon
1 cup fresh lemon juice (about 4 large
   lemons)

1. Bring 3½ cups water, the sugar, and salt to a boil in a large saucepan over high heat, stirring until the sugar is dissolved. Remove the saucepan from the heat, add the tarragon and the sliced lemon, and let stand, covered, for 10 minutes.

2. Meanwhile, puree the honeydew in a blender or a food processor.

3. Pour the syrup and the honeydew puree through a strainer into a pitcher. Stir in the lemon juice. Chill; serve over ice.

And when you *have run out of things to cook with lemons, you can use them as medicine. When you or a loved one is sick with the flu, a very good remedy is* **Hot Lemonade.**

For this you need one big water glass. Into the bottom of it put 1 large spoonful of honey and 1 cinnamon stick. Slice half a lemon into thin slices and put those in too. Now squeeze the remaining lemon half, and 1 more lemon, and put the juice of both into the glass. Fill with hot water, stir, and serve to the sick person with the glass wrapped in a napkin.

While the sick person is recovering, you can tidy up the house using a bottle of lemon furniture polish, and when you are finished you can sit and have a cup of Lemon Zinger tea and a lovely little snack: lemon and poppy seed biscuits and some little Niçoise olives flavored with lemon zest.

—Laurie Colwin, *More Home Cooking*

Whole-Lemon Lemonade

Old recipes for this have you let the mixture sit overnight, but these days, who can wait that long? Using boiling water makes it much faster. This may be my favorite lemonade. It's wonderfully aromatic from the zest.

MAKES ABOUT 4 CUPS

6 small lemons, thinly sliced
1 cup sugar
Pinch of salt

1. Stir the lemons, sugar, and salt together in a large bowl. Mash the slices with a potato masher or a fork. Let stand for 3 hours, stirring occasionally.

2. Add 3 cups boiling water to the lemons and stir well. Cover with a plate and steep for 10 minutes.

3. Pour through a strainer into a pitcher. Chill; serve over ice.

Lemonade Syrup

to make a glass of lemonade, use 2 to 3 table-spoons of this syrup per glass of seltzer or cold water. For a pitcher of lemonade, use ¾ to 1 cup syrup and 4 to 5 cups water. You might also add a spoonful of this to iced tea.

MAKES ABOUT 5 CUPS

2½ cups sugar
Finely grated zest of 4 lemons
Pinch of salt
3 cups fresh lemon juice (about 12 large
    lemons)

1. Bring 1 cup water, the sugar, zest, and salt to a boil in a large saucepan over medium-high heat, stirring until the sugar is dissolved. Boil for 5 minutes, then remove the pan from the heat and let cool to room temperature.

2. Pour the syrup through a strainer into a large glass measure or a bowl. Stir in the lemon juice. Pour the syrup into a large jar or bottle with a tight-fitting lid. The syrup can be stored, refriger-ated, for up to 3 weeks.

3. To use, combine the syrup with cold water, as di-rected in the headnote, and serve over ice.

Lemonade for One

add a slice of lemon as a garnish, if you'd like. For frothy lemonade, make this in a blender, the way they do in the Greek diners in New York City.

SERVES 1

¼ cup fresh lemon juice
2 tablespoons sugar
¾ cup cold sparkling water or tap water

Stir the lemon juice and sugar together in a tall glass until the sugar is dissolved. Add ice cubes and the water, stirring to combine well.

Instant Peppermint Lemonade

We used to have these at Christmastime, but we used oranges. The acid in the citrus fruit makes holes in the peppermint stick so the juice will come through, as though it were a straw: wonderful cold lemon juice coming through a refreshing sweet peppermint stick. Don't use a candy cane: they're not porous enough. You'll need an old-fashioned peppermint stick. The perfect lemon for this is a Meyer. Put the lemon in the freezer for about 30 minutes before cutting the hole in it, so the treat is cold and hot, sweet and tart, all at once.

SERVES 1

1 Meyer or regular lemon, chilled
One 3-inch-long porous peppermint stick

Roll the lemon on a counter to soften the pulp. Make a hole in the top of the lemon, going three-quarters of the way through the fruit. Insert the peppermint stick into the lemon, and suck, until the acid in the lemon begins to make holes in the peppermint stick so the juice will come through.

Lemonade Iced Tea

Use regular or decaffeinated orange pekoe tea, an herb tea like peppermint, or another favorite tea.

MAKES ABOUT 7 CUPS

6 orange-pekoe tea bags
1 lemon, thinly sliced, or zest of 1 lemon,
    removed with a vegetable peeler
Old-fashioned Lemonade (page 151)
Paper-thin lemon slices for garnish

1. Put the tea bags and sliced lemon in a large glass measure or heatproof pitcher and pour 2 cups boiling water over them. Cover and steep for 10 minutes.

2. Remove and discard the tea bags. Let the tea cool to room temperature, and add the lemonade. Chill; serve over ice, garnished with the lemon slices.

Citron Pressé

an active-participation drink. You could serve a small pitcher of Lemoncello (page 164), crème de cassis, or ginger liqueur on the side. In summer, it's a good idea always to have simple syrup in the refrigerator.

SERVES 2

½ cup sugar
Pinch of salt
½ cup fresh lemon juice (about 2 large
    lemons)
2 thin lemon slices
A large bottle of seltzer, chilled, or a carafe
    of cold water

1. Bring ½ cup water, the sugar, and salt to a boil in a small saucepan over high heat, stirring until the sugar is dissolved. Remove the saucepan from the heat and let cool to room temperature.

2. Pour the syrup into a small pitcher and chill.

3. Fill two tall glasses with ice cubes. Divide the lemon juice between the glasses, add a lemon slice to each, and serve the pitcher of simple syrup and the bottle of seltzer on the side, for drinkers to concoct their own combinations. Serve with long spoons.

Lemon Buttermilk

this is amazingly refreshing, and creamy yet low in fat.

SERVES 2

1½ teaspoons finely grated lemon zest
¼ cup fresh lemon juice
2 tablespoons sugar
¼ teaspoon salt
1½ cups buttermilk
2 paper-thin lemon slices

Combine the zest, lemon juice, sugar, and salt in a blender and pulse until smooth. Add the buttermilk and blend well. Serve over ice, garnished with the lemon slices.

drink garnishes

Garnishes for refreshing lemon drinks aren't crucial, but can be a very special treat. Consider these.

- Add extra zest to cold drinks and provide color with lemon wedges, cartwheel slices, or lemon twists.

- Thread cut-up fruits and berries onto skewers. Intertwining them with long strips of lemon zest is especially attractive.

- To make colorful ice cubes, put lemon zest knots, star anise, whole or sliced berries, quartered lemon slices, (unsprayed) lemon blossoms or lemon leaves, herb sprigs, pitted cherries, or kaffir lime leaves in an ice cube tray, fill with water, and freeze. Add to clear beverages and lemonade.

- As if you were serving a margarita, moisten the rim of a glass with lemon and dip in sugar or salt mixed with lemon zest for a zingy treat.

- Rub the edge of a glass with lemon rind to release lemon flavor with every sip.

- Serve hot tea with lemon cartwheel slices studded with whole cloves.

Lemon Barley Water

this is the drink I would take to a desert island. I like it even more than lemonade. It doesn't require as much sugar as lemonade, because the barley adds its own sweetness. This traditional English concoction was originally prepared to nourish the sick, but now it is served as a cool refreshing summer drink, often at tennis matches. Robinsons launched its Patent Barley in 1823, which was sold as a powder. Mixed with water, it was used to combat kidney complaints and fevers. Lemon barley water was first bottled in 1935, and it is still sold in bottles like soda in England. Bruised mint leaves may be added if you like.

MAKES ABOUT 6 CUPS

1 cup pearl barley, preferably organic
½ cup sugar
Zest of 3 lemons, removed with a vegetable
    peeler
Pinch of salt
⅔ cup fresh lemon juice (about 3 large
    lemons)

1. Bring 2 cups water to a boil in a large saucepan over high heat. Add the barley and return to a boil. Reduce the heat and simmer, covered, for 5 minutes.

2. Increase the heat to high, add 4 cups water, the sugar, zest, and salt and return to a boil. Reduce the heat and simmer, covered, for 10 minutes. Remove the saucepan from the heat and let stand, covered, for at least 30 minutes, or until cooled to room temperature.

3. Pour the mixture through a strainer into a pitcher. Add 2 cups water and the lemon juice. Chill; serve over ice.

Lemoncello

Lemoncello, also called limoncello, is a traditional liqueur from Italy's Amalfi Coast and the island of Capri that tastes like fresh lemons. Commercially available all over Italy (I counted nine different brands in the duty-free shop at the Milan airport), it is not often seen here, but it's easy to make at home. Drink it straight or mix it with sparkling wine or water for an aperitif. Or use it in ice cream or sugar syrup, toss it with sliced ripe fruit or berries, or drizzle it over sorbet or ice cream. The vodka takes color and flavor from the zest; if you use 100-proof vodka, it will take less time for the extraction.

MAKES ABOUT 7 CUPS

One 750-ml bottle 80- or 100-proof vodka
Zest of 6 lemons, removed with a vegetable
    peeler
1½ cups sugar

1. Combine the vodka with the zest in a ½-gallon jar and let stand at room temperature, tightly covered, for about 10 days; it is ready when the zest has turned pale and the vodka is a deep yellow color.

2. Pour the liquid through a strainer into a large bowl. Leave the zest in the strainer and place the strainer over a large glass measure or a bowl.

3. Bring 3 cups water and the sugar to a boil in a large saucepan over high heat, stirring until the sugar is dissolved. Boil for 3 minutes. Pour the syrup through the strainer into the glass measure; discard the zest. Cool the syrup completely.

4. Add the syrup to the vodka. Pour the liqueur into a large bottle or smaller decorative bottles with tight-fitting lids. Let stand for 5 days before serving. This is best stored in the freezer and served icy-cold in tiny glasses.

WAYS TO USE LEMONCELLO

- Turn Lemoncello into an ice cream soda using vanilla ice cream and seltzer. Or try it with lemon sorbet.

- Place small scoops of lemon sorbet into Champagne flutes and top with Champagne or other sparkling wine and just a dash of Lemoncello. Garnish with tiny fresh rosemary sprigs, if desired.

- Make what is called Sgroppino in Italy: Combine 1 pint softened vanilla ice cream, 6 tablespoons fresh lemon juice, and ⅓ cup Lemoncello in a blender and blend until smooth and spoonable. Serve in tall stemmed glasses. Or blend 1 pint lemon sorbet, 1 cup sparkling wine, and ¼ cup Lemoncello (or Lemon Vodka, or Grappa, page 166). Pour into six chilled Champagne flutes and garnish each drink with a sprig of fresh mint, fresh currants, or tiny Champagne grapes.

- Make a Bitter Lemon Highball using Lemoncello and bitter lemon soda.

- Serve a Lemon Zinger: Thread 6 long strips of lemon zest removed with a channel knife (see page 14) onto six 7-inch bamboo skewers, with 6 thin cucumber slices, and place in six tall glasses. Combine a bottle of sparkling wine, ¼ cup Lemoncello, and lots of ice cubes in a pitcher. Pour into the glasses.

- Make white sangria with white wine, Lemoncello, and sliced ripe peaches.

I would like a medium dry vodka martini—
with a slice of lemon peel. Shaken and not stirred, please.
—James Bond, from *Dr. No*

Lemon Vodka

feel free to add fresh mint or tarragon sprigs, coriander seeds, or a vanilla bean. My favorite addition is thinly sliced English cucumber; I use two that have been peeled. Or try adding fennel seeds, star anise, or caraway seeds. Try a Lemon Drop cocktail—just blend Lemon Vodka or Gin, Lemon Sorbet and ice cubes in the blender until slushy—it's very refreshing.

MAKES ABOUT 3 CUPS

One 750-ml bottle 80-proof vodka
Zest of 3 lemons, removed with a vegetable
    peeler

1. Combine the vodka and zest in a 1-quart glass jar or bottle. Let stand for 2 weeks.

2. Pour the vodka through a strainer. Discard the zest and return the liquid to the jar. Store tightly covered. This is best stored in the freezer and served icy-cold in tiny glasses.

VARIATIONS:
Substitute tequila, brandy, rum, bourbon, gin, or grappa for the vodka.

adding lemon flavor

LEMONADE AND OTHER DRINKS

- Make lemonade ice cubes and add to iced tea or lemonade.

- Add a couple of strips of lemon zest to freshly brewed coffee before chilling it for iced coffee.

- Flavor mulled wine with lemon zest strips, studded with whole cloves, if you like.

- Make martinis with Lemon Vodka or Gin (page 166).

Lemon Brandy (for flavoring sweet dishes)

Fill any sized wide-necked bottle tightly with the very thin rinds of fresh lemons, and cover them with good brandy; let them remain for a fortnight or three weeks only, then strain off the spirit and keep it well corked for use; a few apricot kernels blanched and imposed with the lemon-rind will give it an agreeable flavor.
 —Eliza Acton, *Modern Cookery* (1861 edition)

breakfast

Lemon-Blueberry Scones
with Lemon Curd

It's very possible that the original use for Lemon Curd was to spread it on just-baked scones. I think it's one of the best ideas anyone has ever had, and I bet you will, too.

MAKES 12 SCONES

⅔ cup heavy cream
1 large egg
1 tablespoon finely grated lemon zest
2 cups all-purpose flour
¼ cup packed light brown sugar
1 tablespoon baking powder
¼ teaspoon salt
4 tablespoons (½ stick) chilled unsalted butter, cut into small pieces
1 cup ripe blueberries, picked over
Lemon Curd (page 228)

1. Position a rack in the middle of the oven. Preheat the oven to 375°F.

2. Whisk together the cream, egg, and zest in a small bowl. Combine the flour, sugar, baking powder, and salt in a large bowl, using your fingers to break up the brown sugar. Work in the butter, with your hands, a pastry blender, or 2 knives, used scissors-fashion, until the mixture resembles coarse meal. Add the blueberries and stir to combine. Slowly pour in the cream mixture, stirring with a fork just until a dough forms; do not overmix. With lightly floured hands, knead the dough, in the bowl, just until it comes together, 8 to 10 times; do not overwork the dough. Divide the dough in half.

3. On a lightly floured surface, form each half into a 6-inch disk about ½ inch thick. Cut each disk into 6 wedges. Separate the wedges and transfer to an ungreased baking sheet.

4. Bake the scones for 22 to 25 minutes, or until golden brown. Cool slightly on a rack. Serve warm, with the Lemon Curd.

Lemon-and-Parsley Baked Eggs

a comforting and very easy Sunday-morning breakfast dish that is very pleasant served with warm buttered toast. Your ramekins don't have to be exactly 4 ounces, but they do need to be at least 4 ounces.

SERVES 4

⅓ cup heavy cream
1 tablespoon finely chopped fresh flat-leaf
    parsley
1½ teaspoons finely grated lemon zest
¼ teaspoon ground coriander
¼ teaspoon salt
Pinch of freshly ground black pepper
4 large eggs

1. Preheat the oven to 325°F. Lightly butter four 4-ounce ramekins or custard cups.

2. Stir together the cream, parsley, zest, coriander, salt, and pepper in a small bowl. Pour about 1 tablespoon of the cream mixture into each ramekin. Break an egg into each ramekin and pour the remaining cream mixture over the eggs.

3. Place the ramekins on a baking sheet for easier handling. Bake for about 18 minutes, for soft yolks, or to desired doneness. Serve hot.

Lemony Ricotta Pancakes with Plum Sauce

although you could serve just about any fruit or berry sauce with these ethereal pancakes, the plum sauce is particularly tasty—and colorful. But if there aren't good plums in the market, try peach, raspberry, apricot, or blueberry sauce, or serve the pancakes with sliced strawberries tossed with a bit of sugar and a pinch of lemon zest.

SERVES 2

3 large ripe purple and/or red plums,
    pitted and chopped
2 tablespoons plus 2 teaspoons sugar
1 teaspoon fresh lemon juice
⅔ cup ricotta cheese
2 large eggs, separated
2 teaspoons finely grated lemon zest
½ teaspoon pure vanilla extract
¼ cup milk
¼ cup plus 2 tablespoons all-purpose flour
¼ teaspoon baking powder
Pinch of salt
Vegetable oil for cooking

1. Combine the plums and 2 tablespoons of the sugar in a medium saucepan and cook over medium-low heat, stirring frequently, until the plums are very soft, about 20 minutes. Let cool slightly. Puree the plums in a food processor. Add the lemon juice and pour through a strainer into a small pitcher. Let stand at room temperature.

2. Process the ricotta, egg yolks, zest, and vanilla in the food processor until smooth, about 2 minutes. Add the milk, flour, the remaining 2 teaspoons sugar, the baking powder, and salt and process until completely blended. Transfer to a bowl.

3. With an electric mixer on medium speed, beat the egg whites in a medium bowl just to stiff peaks. Gently fold the egg whites into the ricotta mixture with a whisk or rubber spatula.

4. Coat a griddle or large skillet with oil and heat over medium heat. Drop the batter by ¼ cupfuls into the skillet and cook until the tops are bubbly and look somewhat dry, 2 to 3 minutes. Turn the pancakes over and cook on the second side until golden brown, about 2 minutes. Transfer to a platter. Serve or keep warm in the oven. Repeat with the remaining batter, using more oil as necessary. Serve the pancakes hot, with the sauce.

Lemony Bread-Pudding French Toast

I'm not crazy about most French toast—I always want it to be crisp and it is often soggy. This recipe solves the problem: it's really a fluffy, custardy bread pudding, under a glorious crisp caramelized crust. It's easy to make, but you do need to put it together the night before. You might prefer fresh fruit to the maple syrup.

SERVES 4 TO 6

2 cups milk
2 tablespoons finely grated lemon zest
6 large eggs
1 teaspoon pure vanilla extract
12 slices homemade-style white bread
　　(see Note)
⅓ cup packed dark brown sugar
4 tablespoons (½ stick) unsalted butter,
　　at room temperature
Pure maple syrup, warmed, for serving

1. Bring the milk just to a boil in a medium saucepan over medium heat. Remove the pan from the heat, add the zest, cover, and let stand for 10 minutes.

2. Pour the milk through a strainer into a glass measure or a bowl and let cool for 15 minutes.

3. Whisk together the eggs and vanilla in a medium bowl. Whisk in the milk.

4. Butter an 8-inch square glass baking dish. Arrange the bread in the pan in 4 stacks of 3 slices each. Pour the milk mixture over the bread and push the bread down to submerge it; let cool to room temperature. Refrigerate, covered, overnight.

5. Preheat the oven to 350°F.

6. Combine the sugar and butter in a small bowl. Spread the butter mixture evenly over the top of the bread.

7. Bake the French toast for 1 hour, or until a paring knife inserted 1 inch from the center comes out clean. Let stand for 10 minutes before serving, with warm maple syrup.

NOTE:
I use Pepperidge Farm Original white bread.

Lemon Yeast-Raised Waffles

These waffles are so light and crisp, after tasting them, you may never go back to regular waffles. They're very easy to make—just throw the batter together the night before, and heat up the waffle iron in the morning.

MAKES TEN 7-INCH ROUND WAFFLES

2 cups milk
4 tablespoons (½ stick) unsalted butter
2 tablespoons finely grated lemon zest
One ¼-ounce package active dry yeast
2 cups all-purpose flour
2 tablespoons light brown sugar
1 teaspoon salt
2 large eggs
¼ teaspoon baking soda
Pure maple syrup, warmed, for serving

1. Bring the milk and butter just to a boil in a medium saucepan over medium-high heat. Remove the pan from the heat, add the zest, cover, and let cool to room temperature. Pour the mixture through a strainer into a medium bowl.

2. Sprinkle the yeast over ½ cup warm water (110° to 115°F) in a large bowl. Let stand for 10 minutes.

3. Add the milk mixture, the flour, sugar, and salt to the yeast mixture and whisk until smooth. Cover and refrigerate overnight.

4. Preheat the oven to 200°F. Preheat a waffle iron.

5. Whisk the eggs and baking soda into the waffle batter. Cook the waffles according to the manufacturer's instructions, or until very crisp. Serve immediately, or keep them warm in the oven, placing the waffles directly on the oven rack to keep them crisp. Serve with the warm maple syrup.

NOTE:
I sometimes leave my waffles in a little longer than the "done" light on my waffle iron indicates, so they'll be darker brown and crisper.

Dutch Baby

dutch babies are puffed pancakes, sliced and served in wedges. Like a soufflé, they need to be enjoyed right out of the oven, so have everything ready. There's no sugar in the batter, so top it with lots of confectioners' sugar, and make sure everyone has lemon wedges handy on their plates. Thanks to my great friend Sabra Turnbull for this recipe.

SERVES 4

3 tablespoons unsalted butter
¾ cup milk, at room temperature
3 large eggs, at room temperature
¾ cup all-purpose flour
Pinch of salt
Confectioners' sugar for dusting
Lemon wedges for serving

1. Preheat the oven to 450°F.

2. Melt the butter in a 10-inch cast-iron skillet over medium heat. Tilt the pan to coat the sides with butter.

3. Meanwhile, put the milk and eggs in a blender, add the flour and salt, and blend just until well combined. Pour the batter into the prepared skillet.

4. Bake for about 12 minutes, or until the pancake is puffed and golden brown. Sprinkle generously with confectioners' sugar and serve immediately, with the lemon wedges on the side.

adding lemon flavor

BREAKFAST

- Drizzle fresh lemon juice over scrambled eggs and top with minced fresh herbs.

- When you heat maple syrup for pancakes, waffles, or whatever, add a few strips of lemon zest; remove them before serving.

- Add a pinch of finely grated lemon zest to your morning oatmeal.

- Add lemon zest and poppy seeds to your favorite pancake batter.

- Add lots of fresh lemon zest to your blueberry muffins.

- Stir finely grated lemon zest into your favorite biscuit dough and serve them for breakfast with Lemonade Marmalade (page 230) or strawberry jam, or both.

- Scramble your eggs with lemon zest, then garnish with snipped fresh chives and slivers of smoked salmon.

sauces

Extra-Lemony
Rosemary Salmoriglio

This Sicilian sauce is wonderful with grilled or roasted fish, poultry, lamb, pork, and beef. You could add a little finely chopped fresh oregano if you like.

MAKES 2/3 CUP

1 teaspoon finely grated lemon zest
¼ cup fresh lemon juice
1 garlic clove, crushed with the side of a
    chef's knife
1 teaspoon fresh rosemary leaves
¼ teaspoon salt
¼ teaspoon coarsely ground black pepper
⅓ cup Lemon Oil (page 214) or olive oil

1. Combine the zest, lemon juice, garlic, rosemary, salt, and pepper in a medium bowl and let stand for 30 minutes.

2. Whisk in the lemon oil. Serve immediately, or cover and let stand at room temperature for up to 4 hours. Whisk the sauce just before serving.

Lemon Butter

Just as wonderful on hot biscuits or scones, pancakes or waffles as on chicken, lamb chops, or fish, this is a very versatile simple sauce.

SERVES 8

8 tablespoons (1 stick) unsalted butter,
    at room temperature
2 teaspoons finely grated lemon zest
1 tablespoon fresh lemon juice
Pinch of salt
Pinch of freshly ground black pepper

1. Stir together all of the ingredients in a small bowl.

2. Shape the mixture into a log about 1½ inches thick on a piece of parchment or wax paper, wrap in the paper, and freeze until firm enough to slice. Or simply cover the bowl and refrigerate; spoon over a dish just before serving.

VARIATIONS:

Lemon-Gremolata Butter
Add 3 tablespoons finely chopped fresh flat-leaf parsley and 1 minced garlic clove. (Good on beef, veal, pork, lamb, fish, chicken, and vegetables.)

Maître d'Hotel Butter
Add 1 tablespoon finely chopped fresh flat-leaf parsley and reduce the lemon juice to 2 teaspoons. (Very versatile, this is great on beef, chicken, pork, veal, or fish.)

Lemon, Mustard, and Thyme Butter
Add 1 tablespoon coarse-grain Dijon mustard and 1 tablespoon fresh thyme leaves, and reduce the zest to a pinch. (Terrific with turkey steaks, broiled pork chops or chicken breasts, or fish steaks.)

Lemon-Anchovy Butter
Add 2 tablespoons finely chopped fresh flat-leaf parsley and 1 tablespoon anchovy paste. (Especially nice on broiled lamb chops, salmon steaks, and veal chops.)

Lemon-Caper Butter
Add 2 tablespoons chopped drained capers, 1 tablespoon finely chopped fresh flat-leaf parsley, and an extra twist of the pepper mill. (Extremely versatile, this is good on beef, veal, pork, fish, and chicken.)

Lemon–Sage Butter
Add 1 teaspoon minced fresh sage. (Perfect with pork and great on tuna steaks.)

Lemon–Tarragon Butter
Add 2 tablespoons finely chopped fresh tarragon. (Wonderful with beef, fish, and chicken.)

Lemon–Chive Butter
Add 2 tablespoons snipped fresh chives. (Perfect with fish, veal, or pork.)

Lemon–Cilantro Butter
Add 2 tablespoons finely chopped fresh cilantro. (Great with poultry, beef, or fish.)

Lemon–Dill Butter
Add 2 tablespoons finely chopped fresh dill. (Serve with pork, fish, or poultry.)

Lemon–Rosemary Butter
Add 2 teaspoons finely chopped fresh rosemary. (Wonderful with lamb.)

Lemon–Mint Butter
Add 2 tablespoons finely chopped fresh mint. (Very good with lamb, pork, or poultry.)

lemon compound butters and butter sauces

There are two kinds of butter sauces. The first, called compound butters, seem more like garnishes than sauces and are simply flavorings stirred into softened butter. They're quick, tasty, and easy to make. These butters are often rolled into a cylinder and refrigerated or frozen, ready to flavor and garnish dishes just before serving. They were traditionally used on broiled items, but now are served on grilled, sautéed, and even steamed foods. Although compound butters may be frozen for several weeks, they should not be refrigerated for longer than 24 hours because the herbs and other flavorings will deteriorate quickly.

Examples of the second type of butter sauce are Brown or Black Butter, Beurre Blanc, and Hollandaise Sauce. Clarified butter is heated to various degrees or stages of brown and flavored with other simple ingredients or softened butter stirred into cooked eggs or a reduction of wine and/or vinegar and aromatics. These sauces are spooned warm over entrées or vegetables.

The primary concern for both types is to use fresh, high-quality, unsalted butter.

Generally, allow about 1 tablespoon of a compound butter and 2 to 4 tablespoons of a butter sauce per serving.

clarified butter

Clarified butter, also called drawn butter, or, in India, ghee, is merely melted butter with the milk solids that form a sediment removed. It is used as a dipping sauce for lobster, to make brown and "black" butter, in Indian cooking, and sometimes in baking. To clarify butter, melt at least ½ pound (2 sticks) unsalted butter in a heavy saucepan over low heat and cook until it is covered with a white froth. Stir the butter and then simmer it, undisturbed, for 20 minutes, or until the milky solids in the bottom of the pan are very lightly browned. Strain the butter through a sieve lined with a double thickness of damp cheesecloth into a bowl, leaving the milky solids in the pan. Pour the butter into a jar and store it, covered, in the refrigerator; it will keep almost indefinitely. For each 1 pound whole butter, you will end up with about 13 ounces (generous 1½ cups) of clarified butter.

Lemon-Garlic Butter

This is particularly good on steak or chicken. If you blanch the garlic, the butter will have a sweeter, milder flavor. Feel free to add finely chopped fresh herbs too.

SERVES 8

2 to 6 garlic cloves, peeled
Pinch of salt
8 tablespoons (1 stick) unsalted butter,
**   at room temperature**
1 tablespoon finely grated lemon zest
1 tablespoon fresh lemon juice
Pinch of freshly ground black pepper

1. If desired, blanch the garlic in a small saucepan of boiling water for 5 to 6 minutes. Drain thoroughly and mash the garlic to a paste using the side of a chef's knife. Or mash the raw garlic to a paste with a pinch of salt.

2. Stir together the butter, garlic, salt (if using blanched garlic), zest, lemon juice, and pepper in a small bowl.

3. Shape the mixture into a log about 1½ inches thick on a piece of parchment or wax paper, wrap in the paper, and freeze until firm enough to slice. Or simply cover the bowl and refrigerate; spoon over a dish just before serving.

Gremolata Brown Butter

In French, brown butter is *beurre noisette*—literally, hazelnut butter—because of its color. Brown and so-called black butters can only be made successfully with clarified butter; otherwise, the milk solids tend to burn, making the resultant sauce speckled and bitter. Use a skillet or saucepan that makes it easy to see the color of the butter, a black pan makes it very difficult. This is excellent with asparagus, broccoli, or fish.

SERVES 4

¼ cup clarified butter (see page 184)
1 tablespoon finely chopped fresh flat-leaf
    parsley
1 teaspoon finely grated lemon zest
1 teaspoon fresh lemon juice
1 garlic clove, minced
Pinch of salt
Pinch of freshly ground black pepper

1. Heat the butter in a small saucepan over medium heat until it is a medium nutty brown color. Immediately pour it into a small glass measure or heatproof bowl and let stand for 3 minutes.

2. Stir in the parsley, zest, lemon juice, garlic, salt, and pepper. Serve immediately.

Lemon Black Butter

Serve black butter (*beurre noir* in French) over fried or poached eggs, skate, fish, or vegetables. The zest is not classic, but it's a fine addition.

SERVES 4 TO 6

¼ cup clarified butter (see page 184)
1 tablespoon finely chopped fresh flat-leaf
    parsley
1 tablespoon finely chopped drained capers
1 teaspoon finely grated lemon zest
2 teaspoons fresh lemon juice
Pinch of salt
Pinch of freshly ground black pepper

Heat the butter in a small saucepan over low heat until dark brown but not black. Remove the pan from the heat and carefully stir in the parsley, capers, zest, lemon juice, salt, and pepper; be prepared: the mixture will spatter. Serve immediately.

Lemon Beurre Blanc

This is a very suave and refined classic French sauce. The only difficulty in preparing it is controlling the heat, and incorporating the butter without letting it melt completely. You can easily do this by keeping the hot saucepan off the burner unless it's absolutely necessary to reheat it slightly. Once you get used to the technique, you may find this is your favorite sauce to make— certainly to eat! Vary the sauce by using all, or some, flavored butter and adding herbs, citrus zest, ginger, or whatever suits your fancy. It's wonderful served with fish, especially shad, as well as with chicken breasts, asparagus, artichokes, and leeks, among many other things. Don't serve it on something just out of the broiler though— the heat from it will break the sauce.

SERVES 4 TO 6

¼ cup plus 2 tablespoons dry white wine
  or dry vermouth
2 tablespoons Lemon Vinegar (page 213) or
  white wine vinegar
1 large shallot, minced
2 teaspoons finely grated lemon zest
8 tablespoons (1 stick) chilled unsalted
  butter, cut into 8 pieces
½ teaspoon fresh lemon juice
Pinch of salt
Dash of hot red pepper sauce

1. Combine the wine, vinegar, shallot, and zest in a small heavy saucepan or skillet and boil over medium-high heat until the liquid is reduced to about 2 tablespoons. Remove the pan from the heat and let cool for 2 minutes.

2. Begin adding the butter one piece at a time, off the heat, whisking after each addition until the sauce is creamy and white, rather like heavy cream; *if* at any point you need a bit more heat to soften the butter, hold the pan briefly over the lowest heat possible—do not let the butter melt, or the sauce will separate. Whisk in the lemon juice, salt, and pepper sauce, pour through a strainer, and serve immediately.

VARIATION:

Lemon Beurre Rouge
Use red wine and red wine vinegar instead of white. Whisk in 2 tablespoons room-temperature heavy cream or crème fraîche after adding the butter. This makes a more stable sauce.

hollandaise

Don't be intimidated—hollandaise may seem mysterious, but it is actually one of the easiest sauces to make. There's only one really important rule: don't let the egg mixture get too hot, or it will scramble. If you think it might be about to get too hot, immediately remove it from the heat and whisk vigorously to cool the eggs. When it cools off a bit, return it to the heat.

Hollandaise is a simple emulsion, which is a mixture of two ingredients that can't usually be smoothly combined. In hollandaise, the two ingredients are butter and eggs. It is necessary to incorporate the butter carefully, adding it slowly so the egg yolks can gradually absorb the fat. Hollandaise sauce is proof that an egg will incorporate an amazing amount of butter, and the result is the smoothest, most luxurious, and unforgettable sauce. Making hollandaise is fun, but not as much fun as serving it to your family and friends on, say, perfectly cooked asparagus or delicate fish.

It's best to make hollandaise no more than 2 hours before serving and to hold it at room temperature.

Hollandaise Sauce

don't be tempted to add too much lemon juice to this irresistible classic sauce; the flavor should be subtle. Use hot red pepper sauce instead of ground pepper so the sauce isn't dotted with black spots. Ethereal and gorgeous, this is better than butter.

SERVES 4

3 large egg yolks
8 tablespoons (1 stick) unsalted butter, melted and cooled slightly
1 tablespoon plus 1 teaspoon fresh lemon juice
¼ teaspoon salt
Dash of hot red pepper sauce

1. Fill a saucepan with about 1½ inches of water and bring to a simmer over medium-low heat.

2. Whisk together the egg yolks and 2 tablespoons water in a stainless-steel bowl that will fit over the saucepan, with plenty of space above the water, until very light and frothy. Place the bowl over the saucepan and whisk constantly until the eggs are warm but not hot. After about 3 to 4 minutes, the mixture will suddenly thicken; continue to whisk vigorously until it is evenly cooked; remove the bowl from the heat if eggs seem too hot. Remove the bowl from the heat and continue to whisk to cool the mixture.

3. Place the butter in a small glass measure or pitcher. Whisking constantly, slowly add the butter in a thin stream, incorporating the butter as it's added. When you've added all the butter, keep whisking for a minute, until the sauce is very thick. Add the lemon juice, salt, and pepper sauce. Pour the sauce through a strainer and store at room temperature until serving.

VARIATIONS:

Saffron Hollandaise

Saffron gives hollandaise a beautiful color, and the flavor is fantastic, great with fish and green vegetables. Just crumble a tiny pinch of saffron threads and add to the yolk mixture at the beginning.

Cold Deviled Hollandaise

Add minced drained cornichons, capers, shallots, parsley, and coarse-grain mustard to warm hollandaise. Chill and serve the sauce cold with cold lobster or chicken.

Flavored-Oil Hollandaise

Use half warm herb or other flavored oil and half butter. Lemon Oil (page 214) made with a mild, buttery olive oil is perfect.

Avgolemono

Very similar to hollandaise, but without the butter. Noted food writer Claudia Roden says it originated in Spain or Portugal, although it's now identified most often with Greece. You can serve this hot or cold, with most seafood and fish, steamed or roasted vegetables, stuffed grape leaves, roast lamb, or roasted potatoes. If you'd like to vary it a bit, add a pinch of ground sumac (see page 40) or crumbled saffron threads, minced fresh dill, and ground coriander seeds, as they do in Turkey.

SERVES 2 TO 4

2 large eggs
1 large egg yolk
2 tablespoons fresh lemon juice
Salt and freshly ground black pepper
½ cup chicken stock or canned low-sodium
    chicken broth

1. Whisk together the eggs, yolk, lemon juice, and salt and pepper to taste in a small bowl.

2. Heat the stock just to a boil in a small saucepan over high heat. Whisking constantly, add ¼ cup of the stock to the egg mixture. Pour the mixture into the stock and cook, whisking constantly, over low heat, until the mixture thickens and your finger leaves a path on the back of a wooden spoon when you draw your finger across it. Immediately transfer the sauce to a bowl, straining it, if desired. The sauce will thicken as it stands. You can keep it warm for 2 hours or chilled for 1 day. Serve warm or cold.

Lemon Aïoli
(Garlic Mayonnaise)

aïoli is very popular in France, where it is sometimes called *"beurre* (butter) *de Provence."* Serve it slightly chilled with fish, cold boiled potatoes or beets, or boiled beef, or as a dip for vegetables. It also makes a great garnish for gazpacho.

SERVES 4 TO 6

Lemon Mayonnaise (page 192)
2 to 6 garlic cloves, minced
Salt
Hot red pepper sauce

Stir together the mayonnaise and garlic in a small bowl until well combined. Season to taste with salt and hot pepper sauce. This will keep, covered and refrigerated, for up to 2 days.

VARIATIONS:
Lemon–Pepper Aïoli
Add lots of freshly cracked black pepper.

Mint Aïoli
Stir in finely shredded fresh mint leaves.

Lemon–Chickpea Aïoli
Add a spoonful of chickpea puree. This makes a great dip.

Lemon Mayonnaise

Of course, you could make lemon mayonnaise using your favorite recipe and Lemon Oil (page 214), adding lemon juice and zest to taste, or you could make it this faster way.

SERVES 4 TO 6

1 cup mayonnaise
1 tablespoon finely grated lemon zest
1 tablespoon fresh lemon juice
2 teaspoons coarse-grain or regular Dijon
   mustard
Pinch of salt
Pinch of freshly ground black pepper

Whisk together the mayonnaise, zest, lemon juice, mustard, salt, and pepper in a small bowl until combined well. This will keep, covered and refrigerated, for up to 1 week.

VARIATIONS:

Lemon-Shallot Mayonnaise
Add minced shallots, raw or cooked.

Lemon-Mustard Mayonnaise
Stir in Dijon and/or whole-grain mustard to taste.

Lemon-Anchovy Mayonnaise
Mash drained anchovies, with garlic if desired, and add to the mayonnaise. Serve with cold seafood.

Lemon-Caviar Mayonnaise
Add about ¼ cup caviar to the mayonnaise, prepared without salt. Serve with poached salmon or other fish.

Lemon-Caper Mayonnaise
Stir in finely grated zest, fresh lemon juice, chopped drained capers, and lots of freshly ground black pepper. Serve with fish or shellfish.

Lemon-Saffron Mayonnaise
Steep a pinch of crumbled saffron threads in the lemon juice before making the mayonnaise.

Gremolata Mayonnaise
Stir in a generous amount of Gremolata (page 198). It's great on cold chicken or fish.

Lemon-Fennel Mayonnaise
Stir in minced fennel bulb and fronds, Pernod, or ground fennel seeds.

Fresh Horseradish Mayonnaise
Stir in grated fresh horseradish just before serving.

Sage-Caper Mayonnaise
Stir in minced fresh sage leaves and capers.

Lemon-Thyme Mayonnaise
Stir in chopped lemon thyme leaves, or lemon zest and chopped regular thyme.

condiments

Lemon Salsa Verde

Salsa verde is a zingy, piquant Italian sauce prepared with fresh parsley, capers, and garlic. Here it is made even better with the addition of lemon zest and Lemon Oil. It's perfect served with grilled meats, fish, and vegetables.

MAKES A SCANT 3/4 CUP

1 garlic clove, peeled
2 cups packed fresh flat-leaf parsley sprigs
¼ cup plus 2 tablespoons Lemon Oil
    (page 214) or olive oil
1 teaspoon finely grated lemon zest
2 tablespoons fresh lemon juice
1 tablespoon drained capers
1 teaspoon Dijon mustard
¼ teaspoon salt
Pinch of freshly ground black pepper

With the motor running, drop the garlic through the feed tube of a small food processor and process until finely chopped. Add the parsley, lemon oil, zest, lemon juice, capers, mustard, salt, and pepper and pulse until smooth. This will keep, covered and refrigerated, for 3 days or more. Stir before serving.

Lemon Persillade

This is remarkable spread over grilled or broiled tomatoes, served as a condiment for meats and poultry, or stirred into pan sauces. You could add some finely chopped shallots.

MAKES ABOUT 1/3 CUP

1 lemon
¼ cup minced fresh flat-leaf parsley
2 tablespoons Lemon Oil (page 214) or
    olive oil
2 tablespoons snipped fresh chives, optional
¼ teaspoon salt
Pinch of freshly ground black pepper

1. Finely grate the zest from the lemon. Cut off a small slice from the top and bottom of the lemon. With a small sharp knife, following the natural curve of the fruit, carefully cut down from the top to the bottom, removing the pith in thick strips. Mince the lemon pulp, discard the seeds.

2. Combine the zest, lemon pulp, parsley, lemon oil, chives, if using, the salt, and pepper in a small bowl and mix well with a fork. This is best used immediately, but it can be stored, covered in the refrigerator, for 1 day.

some uses for gremolata

- Spread it under the skin of a chicken before roasting.

- Sprinkle over roasted cauliflower or asparagus.

- Toss with hot cooked fresh pasta and softened unsalted butter.

- Sprinkle over steamed or sautéed broccoli.

- Toss with roasted beets and Lemon Oil (page 214).

- Stir a bit into a fresh, crisp grated carrot and radish salad, along with a drizzle of Basic Lemon Vinaigrette (page 58).

- Use as a seasoning for grilled peppers, eggplant, and zucchini.

- Sprinkle over fried eggs for a great supper dish. You could also add a pinch of Lemon Dust (page 212).

- Sprinkle over grilled or broiled tomato halves.

Gremolata

You might add minced shallots or use fresh mint, thyme, rosemary, or cilantro along with the parsley.

MAKES ABOUT 3 TABLESPOONS

2 tablespoons finely chopped fresh flat-leaf parsley
1 tablespoon finely grated lemon zest
1 small garlic clove, finely chopped

Chop together all the ingredients until finely minced and well combined. Use immediately.

Cooked Gremolata

Use this version if you're not a fan of raw garlic. It's great for garnishing simple roasted meats and poultry, fish, vegetables, soups, or stews. Or stir it into just-cooked couscous. Add a pinch of minced peeled fresh ginger for an interesting variation. You can chop this by hand, if you prefer.

MAKES ABOUT 3 TABLESPOONS

2 garlic cloves, peeled
¼ cup fresh flat-leaf parsley leaves
2 tablespoons finely grated lemon zest
1 teaspoon Lemon Oil (page 214) or olive oil

1. With the motor running, drop the garlic through the feed tube of a food processor and process until finely chopped. Add the parsley and zest and process until finely chopped.

2. Heat the lemon oil in a small nonstick skillet over medium heat until hot but not smoking. Add the parsley mixture and cook, stirring, for 30 seconds. Use immediately, or transfer to a bowl and let cool to room temperature. This will keep, covered and refrigerated, for 2 days or more.

Chermoula

From Morocco, chermoula is an extraordinary condiment to serve on grilled fish, chicken, or lamb. To toast the spices, heat them in a small dry skillet over medium heat until fragrant.

MAKES ABOUT 1 CUP

1 teaspoon coriander seeds, preferably
    toasted
12 black peppercorns
½ teaspoon cumin seeds, preferably
    toasted
¼ teaspoon crushed hot red pepper flakes
Large pinch of saffron threads
1 small onion, finely chopped
⅓ cup finely chopped fresh flat-leaf
    parsley
Peel of ¼ Preserved Lemon (page 218),
    minced
2 tablespoons juice from Preserved
    Lemons (page 218)
2 tablespoons Lemon Oil (page 214) or
    olive oil
2 tablespoons finely chopped fresh cilantro
1 garlic clove, minced
1 teaspoon sweet paprika

Finely grind the coriander, peppercorns, cumin, pepper flakes, and saffron in a spice grinder or in a mortar and pestle. Transfer to a small bowl and stir in the onion, parsley, preserved lemon peel and juice, lemon oil, cilantro, garlic, and paprika. This will keep, covered and refrigerated, for 2 weeks or more.

Tomato Salsa with Lemon

You may never go back to plain salsa. The lemon really enhances the tomato, makes the flavor come alive, and adds a clean refreshing dimension. This is particularly good with grilled meats, fish, poultry, and tortilla chips. You could also add some chopped olives and capers.

MAKES ABOUT 1 1/2 CUPS

1 lemon
3 ripe medium tomatoes, seeded and finely
   chopped
2 tablespoons finely chopped fresh basil or
   flat-leaf parsley
1 tablespoon Lemon Oil (page 214) or olive
   oil
¼ teaspoon salt
Pinch of freshly ground black pepper

1. Finely grate the zest from the lemon. Cut off a small slice from the top and bottom of the lemon. With a small sharp knife, following the natural curve of the fruit, carefully cut down from the top to the bottom, removing the pith in thick strips. Finely chop the lemon pulp, discard the seeds.

2. Stir together the lemon zest, lemon pulp and any juice, the tomatoes, basil, lemon oil, salt, and pepper in a bowl. Serve immediately, or refrigerate, covered, for up to 24 hours. Serve at room temperature.

Moroccan-Style Lemon, Red Onion, and Parsley Salsa

This clean-tasting, refreshing salsa is good on just about anything, including meats, poultry, and eggs. Though it's perfect as it is, for variety you could add cilantro, a bit of Lemon Oil (page 214), minced Preserved Lemon peel (page 218), ground cumin, or garlic.

MAKES ABOUT 1 CUP

4 small lemons
1 large mild red onion, cut into ¼-inch
**   dice**
½ cup finely chopped fresh flat-leaf parsley
¾ teaspoon salt
Pinch of freshly ground black pepper

1. Cut off a small slice from the top and bottom of each lemon. With a small sharp knife, following the natural curve of the fruit, carefully cut down from the top to the bottom, removing both the rind and the pith in thick strips; discard. Slip a small sharp knife alongside the membranes on both sides of one section, freeing it, and let it fall into a bowl. Repeat with the remaining sections, removing the seeds as you go and reserving the juice. Squeeze the juice from the membranes into the bowl. Cut the sections into ½-inch pieces.

2. Stir in the onion, parsley, salt, and pepper. Serve immediately.

Sweet-and-Hot
Lemon Confit

hot and sweet is just how a condiment should be. Serve this with the Thanksgiving turkey, roast chicken, ham, or whatever your heart desires.

MAKES ABOUT 1 CUP

6 lemons
1 cup sugar
2 slices crystallized ginger, cut into long
    thin strips
1 whole star anise
½ teaspoon crushed hot red pepper flakes

1. Remove the zest from the lemons with a vegetable peeler and cut it into needle-thin strips. Cut off a small slice from the top and bottom of each lemon. With a small sharp knife, following the natural curve of the fruit, carefully cut down from the top to the bottom, removing the pith in thick strips. Chop the lemon pulp, discard the seeds.

2. Add the lemon zest to a saucepan of boiling water and boil for 8 minutes. Drain in a colander, rinse under cold running water, and drain again.

3. Bring the sugar and ½ cup water to a boil in a medium saucepan over high heat, stirring until the sugar is dissolved. Add the lemon zest and pulp, the ginger, and star anise and return to a boil. Reduce the heat to low and simmer until the zest is softened and the liquid is very slightly caramelized, beginning to turn pale amber, about 30 minutes. Remove the pan from the heat and stir in the pepper flakes. Let cool; the confit will thicken as it stands. This will keep, covered and refrigerated, for 2 weeks or more. Serve cold.

Lemon, Mint, and Olive Relish

enjoy this as a topping for grilled or broiled meats, poultry, or fish.

MAKES ABOUT 1 1/4 CUPS

2 garlic cloves, thinly sliced
½ teaspoon cumin seeds
½ teaspoon fennel seeds
¼ teaspoon crushed hot red pepper flakes
½ cup thinly sliced mild red onion
16 green Mediterranean olives, pitted
   and chopped
8 thin lemon slices, each cut into 8 wedges
2 tablespoons Lemon Oil (page 214) or olive
   oil
1 teaspoon salt
2 tablespoons finely shredded fresh mint leaves

1. Combine ½ cup water, the garlic, cumin, fennel, and pepper flakes in a small saucepan and bring to a boil over medium-high heat. Reduce the heat and simmer until the liquid is reduced to ¼ cup, about 5 minutes. Transfer to a bowl and let cool to room temperature.

2. Stir in the onion, olives, lemons, lemon oil, and salt. Let stand for at least 10 minutes and up to 2 hours before serving.

3. Just before serving, stir in the mint.

Vietnamese-Style Lemon Dipping Sauce

Several of my favorite Vietnamese restaurants offer this sauce with many of their specialty dishes, either in addition to or in place of fish sauce or hot pepper seasoning. Strong and intense, yet utterly simple, it's absolutely necessary for dipping glazed quail, and very good with roasted poultry. This amount should be enough for 6 people. Do make it just before serving.

MAKES 1/4 CUP

¼ cup fresh lemon juice
1 teaspoon kosher salt
1 teaspoon freshly ground black pepper

Combine the lemon juice, salt, and pepper in a small bowl and stir until the salt is dissolved. Serve at room temperature.

Lemon-Ginger Dipping Sauce

Another great Asian-style table condiment. Besides being the perfect sauce for dumplings, this is great with fried shrimp and calamari. And once you taste it, you'll think of many other uses. Finely grate a 1-inch piece of ginger (a Microplane zester is perfect; see page 12) and then squeeze it between your fingers to get the juice. Toast the sesame seeds in a skillet over medium heat until fragrant.

MAKES ABOUT 3/4 CUP

½ cup light soy sauce
1 tablespoon plus 1 teaspoon fresh lemon juice
1 tablespoon finely chopped fresh cilantro
1 tablespoon fresh ginger juice
1½ teaspoons sesame seeds, toasted

Stir together all the ingredients in a small bowl. The sauce will keep, covered and refrigerated, for 3 days or more. Serve at room temperature.

adding lemon flavor

CONDIMENTS

- Thinly sliced seeded cucumber tossed with finely grated lemon zest and finely shredded fresh mint leaves makes a great relish for fish.

- Add fresh lemon juice, zest, or whole slices (with the peel) to any barbecue sauce for a fresher flavor.

- Make a relish with chopped thinly sliced lemons, honey, slivered garlic, and fresh thyme. Use sparingly with roasted meats; it's especially good with pork.

- Cook together balsamic vinegar, brown sugar, lots of lemon zest strips, and a few allspice berries, and pour over dried figs. Store at room temperature, in a tightly covered jar. Use the liquid to deglaze pans after sautéing chicken or pork, and serve the figs on the side.

- Stir up a fresh lemon salsa with chopped paper-thin lemon slices, fresh ripe tomato, yellow bell pepper, roasted poblano chile, and cilantro.

- Try a salsa with chopped Preserved Lemon peel (page 218), chopped ripe tomato, cumin, a pinch of ground cardamom, and lots of chopped cilantro.

- Pitted and chopped black Mediterranean olives, chopped tomato, chopped anchovies, drained capers, chopped parsley, and fresh lemon zest make a great salsa.

- Make a relish with chopped dried dates, lemon zest, minced cilantro, and toasted pine nuts to serve with meats.

pantry

Lemon Salt

Lemon salt is a great seasoning to keep near your stove, ready to spice up a simple dish of almost any type. Use it with vegetables, poultry, sauces, or whatever you're cooking that you think might need a little extra spunk.

MAKES ABOUT 2 TABLESPOONS

1 tablespoon Oven-Dried Lemon Zest (page 15)
2 tablespoons kosher salt

Grind the dried lemon zest in a spice grinder until very fine. Transfer to a small bowl and stir in the salt. Transfer to a small jar and store, tightly covered, at room temperature. This will keep for several months.

Lemon-Coriander Salt

Here's another stove-side condiment for seasoning many of your favorite foods; it will give them a mysterious extra dimension. I love it on roast chicken or fish, or pan-fried steak, and in soups.

MAKES A SCANT $^1/_4$ CUP

1 tablespoon Oven-Dried Lemon Zest (page 15)
1 tablespoon coriander seeds, preferably toasted (see note)
2 tablespoons kosher salt

Grind the dried lemon zest and coriander in a spice grinder until very fine. Transfer to a small bowl and stir in the salt. Transfer to a small jar and store, tightly covered, at room temperature. This will keep for several months.

NOTE:
Toast the coriander seeds in a small dry skillet over medium heat for about 3 minutes, or until fragrant.

Gremolata Salt

great for seasoning fish, poultry, roasted vegetables, dips, and sauces. Try it on popcorn, with a little hot melted butter or warm Lemon Oil (page 214).

MAKES A SCANT 1/2 CUP

2 small garlic cloves, peeled
¼ cup plus 2 tablespoons kosher salt
¼ cup loosely packed fresh flat-leaf parsley
  leaves
1 tablespoon finely grated lemon zest

1. Preheat the oven to 175°F.

2. With the motor running, drop the garlic through the feed tube of a small food processor and process until finely chopped. Add 1 tablespoon of the salt, the parsley, and zest and process until finely chopped. Transfer to a bowl and stir in the remaining ¼ cup plus 1 tablespoon salt.

3. Spread the mixture evenly on a large baking sheet and dry it in the oven for 1 hour, stirring several times to break up any lumps. Let cool to room temperature.

4. Transfer to a small jar and store, tightly covered, at room temperature. This will keep for several months; shake well before using.

Lemon Pepper

those supermarket lemon pepper blends have too much undesirable stuff in them—like tons of salt, old garlic, and preservatives. This is pure and simple and very handy for seasoning all types of dishes. Use it as you would coarsely cracked black peppercorns.

MAKES ABOUT 3 TABLESPOONS

¼ **cup finely grated lemon zest**
1½ **teaspoons coarsely cracked black**
   peppercorns

1. Preheat the oven to 200°F.

2. Spread the lemon zest evenly on a baking sheet and dry in the oven for 20 minutes, turning with a spatula twice, or until it is dry and has turned from yellow to orange. Transfer to a small bowl and let cool to room temperature.

3. Stir in the pepper, transfer to a small jar, and store, tightly covered, at room temperature. This will keep for several months.

Life is a *difficult thing in the country, and it requires a good deal of forethought to steer the ship, when you live twelve miles from a lemon.*

—Sydney Smith

Lemon Dust

this is absolute heaven, my favorite garnish and mood elevator. Just dust it over fried eggs and you'll see what I mean. I don't think there's a dish it wouldn't improve, but I may be prejudiced. It was inspired by Orange Dust in Jean-Georges Vongerichten's book *Cooking at Home with a Four-Star Chef* (Broadway Books, 1998). Make sure you grind the zest as fine as possible—and let the spice grinder sit for a few minutes before removing the cover, so you don't lose your precious dust to the air. Wow, is this fragrant, the very essence of lemon. You only need to use a very little, so be stingy.

MAKES ABOUT 3 TABLESPOONS

Zest of 4 lemons, removed with a vegetable peeler
½ cup sugar
½ teaspoon vegetable oil

1. Preheat the oven to 300°F.

2. Bring 1 cup water, the zest, and sugar to a boil in a medium saucepan over high heat. Reduce the heat to low and simmer for 10 minutes. Drain the zest and dry on paper towels. (Discard the syrup.)

3. Line a large baking sheet with aluminum foil and grease the foil with the oil. Spread the zest on the foil in a single layer, with the pieces not touching one another. Bake for about 18 minutes, or until the zest is dry. Watch it carefully, and do not let it brown; if it begins to brown before it is dry, reduce the oven temperature to 275°. Remove the pan from the oven and cool to room temperature.

4. Grind the zest in a spice grinder as fine as possible. Transfer to a small jar and store, tightly covered, at room temperature. The dust will be at its best for 2 weeks. Its intensity will decline after that, but it will keep for a long time.

Lemon Vinegar

Seasoned Japanese rice vinegar, seasoned with sugar and salt, is available in Asian markets, specialty foods stores, and many supermarkets. I use Marukan brand. You could substitute apple cider or balsamic, white wine, or red wine vinegar. Add whatever other seasonings you like; herbs such as parsley and thyme are always good.

   To give this as a gift, pour the vinegar into a beautiful bottle and add a long spiral of lemon zest threaded onto a bamboo skewer. I love to splash just a bit of this into a glass of seltzer over ice; it makes a very refreshing drink.

MAKES 1 CUP

1 cup seasoned rice vinegar
2 tablespoons finely grated lemon zest

1. Place the vinegar and zest in a glass jar, seal tightly, and let stand at room temperature for at least 1 week, shaking occasionally.

2. Pour the vinegar through a strainer into a glass measure or a bowl and discard the zest. Transfer to a jar and store indefinitely, tightly covered, at room temperature.

**some uses for
lemon oil**

- Use it to make marinated mushrooms.

- Drizzle over grilled or roasted asparagus and add a pinch of kosher salt.

- Use as a dip for crusty bread.

- Use as a dip for artichokes.

- Add to your favorite white bean salad.

- Drizzle over the top of fresh tomato soup.

- Drizzle over pasta just before serving.

- Drizzle over grilled or roasted fish.

- Use in risotto.

- Make bagna cauda with it.

- Add it to your favorite panzanella recipe.

- Cook bitter greens and garlic in it and top with toasted pine nuts.

- Toss roasted potatoes with the oil, fresh sage or rosemary, and kosher salt and freshly ground black pepper.

- Drizzle over squares of feta cheese and serve with toasted pita bread.

Lemon Oil

The uses for this are almost limitless. Fragrant but not overwhelming, it adds a subtle layer of lemon flavor whenever you add it to a dish. Cook your vegetables in it or use it to fry eggs or to make mayonnaise or vinaigrettes. Toss it with pasta, or baste grilled or roasted foods, especially seafood, with it. Add it to stir-fries and to marinades. Add a few fresh unsprayed lemon leaves if you have them, or a sprig of fresh rosemary, lemon thyme, basil, or sage sprigs; a minced stalk of lemongrass; a handful of green Mediterranean olives; or imported bay leaves, peppercorns, coriander seeds, chives, hot red pepper flakes, allspice berries, a cinnamon stick, lots of flat-leaf parsley, a large pinch of crumbled saffron threads, or fennel seeds. You can use part extra-virgin and part regular olive oil, but I've found that the stronger the oil's flavor is, the longer the mixture needs to steep for the lemon flavor to come through.

MAKES I CUP

1 cup extra virgin olive oil, olive oil, grapeseed oil, or vegetable oil
3 tablespoons finely grated lemon zest

1. Place the oil and zest in a glass jar, cover tightly, and refrigerate for at least 3 weeks, shaking occasionally.

2. Pour the oil through a strainer into a glass measure or a bowl and discard the zest. Transfer to a jar, cover tightly, and refrigerate.

- Brush on scallions or other vegetables before grilling.

- Marinate fish or shrimp in it before grilling.

- Add to a quick couscous salad.

- Use to dress a spinach salad.

- Drizzle over the goat cheese in a warm goat cheese salad.

- Dress a salad of paper-thin sliced fennel with Lemon Oil, parsley, lemon juice, garlic, salt, and pepper.

preserved lemons

Preserved lemons are one of the best things about Moroccan food. They are easy to make, last a long time, and add a flavor like no other to a great number of dishes. They can be stored for up to a year in the refrigerator (although they don't really need to be refrigerated except in unusually hot and humid weather). Occasionally, some harmless white crystals may form on top of the lemons. Never dip your fingers into the jar. Remove the lemons with a very clean spoon or tongs. A greasy spoon might spoil the pickling mixture.

You can make the lemons using boiling water instead of lemon juice, but they will take longer to mature. If you do make them with boiling water, top them off with a thin layer of olive oil to protect them. Meyer lemons can be preserved in the same way. (See page 225 for a recipe for Sweet Preserved Lemons.)

Traditionally, only the peel of preserved lemons is used; the pulp is removed and discarded. But give both the pulp and the juice a try as an addition to vinaigrettes, salads, condiments, soups, drinks, and stews. When a recipe in this book calls for preserved lemon peel and its juice, use the Classic Moroccan-Style Preserved Lemons.

Quick Preserved Lemons

This was adapted from an untraditional recipe of Claudia Roden's, in her stunning book *Tamarind & Saffron* (published in England by Viking). These take only 4 days to mature and are not quite as salty or tangy as lemons preserved with the pulp attached—which means some people will like them better.

4 lemons
¼ cup kosher salt
1 teaspoon coriander seeds, optional
¼ teaspoon black peppercorns, optional
**1 cup olive or vegetable oil, or as needed
 to cover**

1. With a sharp knife, make 8 lengthwise slits in each lemon, going just through the zest and pith, not into the pulp. Put the lemons and salt in a large saucepan and cover with boiling water. Use the lid from a smaller pan to keep the lemons submerged and boil until the peels are very soft, about 20 minutes. Remove the lemons from the liquid, drain, and let cool to room temperature.

2. Cut the lemons lengthwise into quarters. With a small spoon, scoop out and discard the pulp. Dry the peel between layers of paper towels, then let dry on a wire rack for 30 minutes.

3. Scrape out any remaining pith from the peel. Cut the peel into long thin strips and pack into a glass jar, with the coriander and peppercorns, if using. Cover with the olive oil. Let the lemons sit for at least 4 days before using. They can be stored at room temperature for 4 months or more.

Cut 3 large juicy *lemons across the top and stuff salt into them; set them upright in a dish before the fire and turn them every day. When they become dry, roast them in a Dutch oven until they become brown. Boil a quart of vinegar, with a quarter of a pound of anchovies, without the bones and scales (but do not wash them), four blades of mace, half a nutmeg sliced, and a spoonful of white pepper; boil gently ten minutes; then pour it, boiling hot, on the lemons, in a stone jar; and cover close. Let it stand six weeks, then put it into quarter-pint flat bottles. It is excellent for made dishes and the lemon eats well.*
—The Book of Domestic Cookery (1829)

Classic Moroccan-Style Preserved Lemons

I add green olives, red chiles, coriander seeds, peppercorns, bay leaves, and allspice berries to my preserved lemons. You can choose whatever you'd like. See page 219 for other possible additions that add lots of flavor but are never overwhelming.

6 large lemons
¼ cup plus 2 tablespoons kosher salt
3 cups fresh lemon juice (about 12 large lemons), or as needed to cover

1. Place the lemons in a ½-gallon jar; it should be about three-quarters full. Cover the lemons with water, leaving some air space at the top. Let stand, tightly covered, for 3 days, changing the water every day.

2. Drain and dry the lemons. Cut each lengthwise into quarters from the blossom end to within ½ inch of the stem end, taking care to leave the 4 pieces joined. Place a couple of teaspoons of the salt in the same very clean jar. Divide the remaining salt among the lemons, placing it on the pulp. "Reshape" the lemons and pack into the jar, pushing them down so that their juices are squeezed out, alternating them with any of the optional ingredients, if using. Add any remaining salt.

3. Cover the lemons with the lemon juice, leaving some air space. You may need to put something into the jar to keep the lemons submerged; I use a small porcelain cup. Cover with the lid, shake the mixture, and let stand at room temperature in a cool spot for at least 3 weeks, shaking the jar daily. The lemons are ready when the rind is soft. If any mold appears on top of the juice, just discard it—it's harmless.

4. To use, remove the lemons from the brine, remove and discard the pulp, and rinse the peel.

OPTIONAL ADDITIONS:

- ½ to 1 cup cracked green Mediterranean olives
- 8 fresh (unsprayed) lemon leaves
- 6 cardamom pods
- 2 or 3 imported bay leaves
- 1 cinnamon stick
- 2 or more whole cloves
- 1 tablespoon coriander seeds
- 1 teaspoon cumin seeds
- 1 teaspoon fennel seeds
- 12 to 18 peppercorns
- 12 allspice berries
- 1 or 2 fresh or dried red chiles
- 3 tablespoons honey

uses for preserved lemons

- Add julienne strips of peel to green salads.
- Add minced to your favorite tabbouleh recipe.
- Make a salad with sliced navel oranges topped with a mixture of finely chopped preserved lemon peel, paper-thin slices of mild red onion, black olives, and chopped cilantro.
- Toss roasted yellow bell peppers, cut into long thin strips, with olive oil, lemon juice, minced fresh flat-leaf parsley, and chopped preserved lemon peel; add minced garlic if you like.
- Pat a mixture of kosher salt and cumin over a leg of lamb before roasting. Serve with couscous studded with almonds, currants, and julienned preserved lemon peel.
- Toss green beans with minced garlic and preserved lemons while sautéing in olive oil. Add roasted red pepper strips, if desired.
- Add finely chopped preserved lemon peel to a vinaigrette used to dress roasted or grilled red peppers. Add some capers, too.
- Make a flavored butter or mayonnaise with minced preserved lemon peel.
- Use the liquid from preserved lemons in salad dressings instead of vinegar, to add flavor to fish or chicken tagines, or in Bloody Marys.

Another Quick Preserved Lemon

like the recipe on page 216, this was also inspired by Claudia Roden. Freezing lemons before preserving them hastens the process. They are fabulously delicious and ready to use very quickly.

4 lemons
¼ cup kosher salt
1¼ cups olive and/or vegetable oil, or as needed
    to cover

1. Cut each lemon lengthwise into 8 wedges. Place in a self-sealing plastic bag and freeze for 24 hours.

2. Transfer the lemons to a colander set over a bowl. Sprinkle with the salt, toss, and let drain for 4 hours.

3. Pack the lemon wedges into a wide-mouth 1-quart jar and cover with the olive oil. Store in a cool dry place for 2 to 3 days before using. Once they've been opened, keep refrigerated. They will last, tightly covered in the refrigerator, for 6 months or more.

Quick Preserved Lemons with Shallots and Garlic

this was adapted from a recipe of chef Thomas Colicchio of New York's Gramercy Tavern (from an article by Elizabeth Scheneider in *Food Arts* magazine). They must be refrigerated because of the garlic. The gorgeous yellow lemons combined with the bright purple shallots is a stunning combination. You can use all of the components— the oil, lemons, garlic, and shallots—together or separately.

4 lemons
¼ cup kosher salt
1 tablespoon plus 1 teaspoon sugar
3 shallots, thinly sliced
3 garlic cloves, thinly sliced
1½ cups olive oil or vegetable oil, or as
    needed to cover

1. Bring the lemons and enough water to cover to a boil in a medium saucepan over high heat and boil for 1 minute. Drain and dry the lemons.

2. Remove the tops and bottoms of each lemon. Cut each lemon crosswise into ¼-inch-thick slices and discard the seeds. Spread the slices on a large baking sheet, sprinkle with the salt and sugar, cover, and refrigerate overnight.

3. Transfer the lemon slices and any accumulated liquid to a medium bowl. Stir in the shallots and garlic, cover, and refrigerate overnight.

4. Transfer the mixture to a wide-mouth 1-quart jar. Pour in olive oil to cover and refrigerate overnight before using. These will last, tightly covered in the refrigerator, for 6 months or more.

Greek-Style Olive Oil—Preserved Lemons

I love to add thin strips of these lemon slices to long-cooking dishes like soups and stews, to quickly sautéed vegetable dishes, and to fish dishes, however they're prepared.

4 lemons
¼ cup kosher salt
Fresh or dried bay leaves, marjoram,
    oregano, and/or coriander seeds, optional
1¼ cups olive oil, or as needed to cover

1. Place the lemons in a wide-mouth 1-quart jar; it should be about three-quarters full. Cover with water, leaving some air space at the top. Let stand, tightly covered, for 3 days, changing the water every day.

2. Drain and dry the lemons. Trim the ends from each lemon. Cut the lemons crosswise into ¼-inch-thick slices, and discard the seeds. Spread the slices out in a single layer on a large baking sheet and sprinkle with the salt. Cover and refrigerate for 24 hours.

3. Layer the slices in a 1-quart glass jar with the herbs and/or coriander, if using. Add any liquid that accumulated on the baking sheet. Pour over enough olive oil to cover. Let stand, tightly covered, in a cool spot for at least 3 weeks, shaking the jar occasionally. Refrigerate the lemons after opening. They will keep, tightly covered and refrigerated, for 6 months or more.

Lemon Sugar

keep lemon sugar on hand to serve in hot or iced tea or coffee, to use in baked goods and frostings, to make cinnamon toast, or to sprinkle over sugar cookies, fruits, or hot cereal. It has a lovely subtle perfume. Grind a pinch of anise seeds or half a vanilla bean with it, if you like. Or you could layer the sugar in the jar with aromatic treats like rose petals, cinnamon sticks, or scented geranium leaves.

MAKES I CUP

2 tablespoons finely grated lemon zest
1 cup sugar

1. Preheat the oven to 200°F.

2. Stir together the zest and sugar on a large baking sheet until the zest is well coated. Spread the mixture out evenly and bake, stirring occasionally with a fork, for 15 minutes. Remove from the oven and let cool to room temperature.

3. Pulse the mixture in a food processor until finely ground. Transfer to a jar and store, tightly covered, at room temperature. The sugar will keep for 3 months or more.

Lemon Brown Sugar

this takes a bit longer to make than regular Lemon Sugar (page 223) because brown sugar contains more moisture. You'll discover this has almost infinite uses. Here's one: line a baking sheet with parchment paper, spread whole ripe strawberries on it in a single layer and sprinkle them with the sugar. Roast in the center of a 375°F oven for 30 minutes, until softened. Serve warm over ice cream.

MAKES I CUP

2 tablespoons finely grated lemon zest
1 cup packed light brown sugar

1. Preheat the oven to 200°F.

2. Stir together the zest and sugar on a large baking sheet, breaking up any lumps, until the zest is well coated. Spread the mixture out evenly and bake, stirring occasionally with a fork, for 20 minutes; it will still look damp in spots when you remove it from the oven. Let cool to room temperature.

3. Pulse the mixture in a food processor until finely ground. Transfer to a jar and store, tightly covered, at room temperature. The sugar will keep for 3 months or more.

Lemon Honey

Spread this on biscuits, scones, or toast or put it in your tea or on hot cereal. Use it anytime you would regular honey.

MAKES ABOUT 1/2 CUP

2 lemons
½ cup honey

1. Bring the lemons and enough water to cover to a boil in a medium saucepan over high heat and boil for 1 minute. Remove the lemons with a slotted spoon and let cool slightly. When cool enough to handle, grate the zest from the lemons.

2. Stir together the zest and honey in a small saucepan and bring to a boil over medium heat. Remove the pan from the heat and let cool to room temperature.

3. Transfer the honey to a jar and store, tightly covered, at room temperature. The honey will keep for 4 months or more.

Lemon Extract

far, far better than the artificial lemon extract sold in supermarkets. Use whenever lemon extract is called for.

MAKES 1/2 CUP

1 lemon
½ cup brandy

1. Bring the lemon and enough water to cover to a boil in a medium saucepan over high heat, and boil for 1 minute. Remove the lemon with a slotted spoon and let cool slightly. When cool enough to handle, remove the zest from the lemon with a vegetable peeler.

2. Place the zest and brandy in a jar. Cover tightly and let stand at room temperature for 2 weeks.

3. Pour the brandy through a strainer into a bowl; discard the zest. Transfer to a small jar and store, tightly covered, at room temperature. The extract will keep for a year or more.

Sweet Preserved Lemons

drizzle the syrup from these lemons over fruit salad or into beverages, or serve it as an after-dinner liqueur. Use thin strips of the peel or finely diced peel to flavor muffins, cakes, and desserts or dessert sauces. Or use it to make Sweet Gremolata (page 226).

4 lemons
1 vanilla bean, split lengthwise
1 star anise
1¼ cups vodka, or as needed to cover
1 cup sugar

1. Bring a large saucepan of water to a boil over high heat. Add the lemons, return to the boil, and boil for 1 minute. Drain and dry the lemons.

2. Cut each lemon lengthwise into quarters from the blossom end to within ½ inch of the stem end, taking care to leave the 4 pieces joined.

3. Place the vanilla bean and star anise in a wide-mouth 1-quart jar. Pack the lemons into the jar.

4. Combine the vodka and sugar in the rinsed-out saucepan. Cook over low heat, stirring, until the sugar is dissolved; do not boil. Pour the syrup over the lemons. Add more vodka to cover the lemons if necessary. Cover tightly and refrigerate for at least 2 weeks before using, shaking the jar occasionally.

5. The lemons will keep, tightly covered in the refrigerator, for 4 months or more.

Sweet Gremolata

make this just before serving. You can, though, chop the lemon peel and ginger several hours ahead; keep them tightly covered. This is great served sprinkled over a fruit salad, a bowl of berries, or a warm fruit compote.

MAKES ABOUT 3 TABLESPOONS

2 tablespoons chopped fresh mint
1 tablespoon chopped peel of Sweet Preserved
**   Lemons (page 225)**
1 slice crystallized ginger, chopped

Chop together all of the ingredients until minced and well combined.

Candied Lemon Slices

here's a great treat to have on hand in your refrigerator. You can use the syrup under, in, and over desserts. The slices make a stunning, very professional looking garnish for desserts, or you could serve just a dab of the slices and the syrup alongside a roast chicken or pork tenderloin. A Feemster Slicer (see page 19), a mandoline, or a very sharp knife is essential here. Also very helpful is a Polder probe thermometer.

MAKES I CUP SLICES (PLUS SYRUP)

4 lemons
2 cups sugar
1 cinnamon stick
1 imported bay leaf or ½ California
**   bay leaf**
2 pieces whole star anise
8 black peppercorns

1. Preheat the oven to 175°F.

2. Trim off the ends of the lemons and cut the lemons into ⅛-inch-thick slices; discard the seeds. Place the slices in a single layer, not touching each other, on a large baking sheet.

3. Dry the lemons in the oven for 2½ hours, or until they are almost completely dry. Remove from the oven.

4. Meanwhile, combine 2 cups water, the sugar, cinnamon, bay leaf, star anise, and peppercorns in a large saucepan and bring to a boil over high heat. Reduce the heat and simmer for 20 minutes.

5. Add the lemon slices to the syrup, return to a simmer, and simmer until the lemons are slightly translucent, about 5 minutes. Remove the lemons with a slotted spoon and place them in a glass jar.

6. Increase the heat to high and boil the syrup until the temperature reaches 220°F on a candy thermometer. Let the syrup cool for 5 minutes.

7. Pour the syrup over the lemon slices. Let cool to room temperature, cover, and refrigerate. The slices will keep, tightly covered in the refrigerator, for 4 months or more.

Curd

No commercially made lemon curd approaches the lemony lusciousness of the homemade version. Lemon curd is a bright yellow, tart, translucent, tangy-sweet, creamy custard made with butter instead of milk. Something like a preserve, lemon curd contains eggs and butter instead of pectin as a thickening agent. It has a shorter shelf life than preserves, but it will keep for several weeks, tightly covered, in the refrigerator, but only if forgotten—usually it disappears rapidly, often by the spoonful at midnight. It is popular in Great Britain on toasted bread or cake, scones fresh out of the oven, or muffins, on cakes, and in tart fillings, as well as in trifle. Served hot or cold, this rich, thick sauce is excellent over fresh fruit, gingerbread, or angel food or pound cake.

This recipe uses the yolks only, no egg whites, which makes it much easier to prepare, as you don't have to use a double boiler. Lemon Curd is really the most useful of pantry staples, and I often make a double batch.

MAKES ABOUT 1¹/₂ CUPS

8 tablespoons (1 stick) unsalted butter
¾ cup sugar
3 tablespoons finely grated lemon zest
½ cup fresh lemon juice (about 2 large lemons)
Pinch of salt
6 large egg yolks

1. Melt the butter in a heavy medium saucepan over medium-low heat. Remove the pan from the heat and whisk in the sugar, zest, lemon juice, and salt. Whisk in the yolks until smooth.

2. Cook the mixture, whisking constantly, until it thickens and your finger leaves a path on the back of a wooden spoon when you draw your finger across it; do not allow the curd to boil.

3. Immediately pour the curd through a strainer into a bowl. Let cool to room temperature, whisking occasionally, then refrigerate, tightly covered, until ready to serve. Lemon curd will keep for 3 weeks in the refrigerator and for 3 months in the freezer.

Candied Julienne Zest

this recipe is similar to Candied Lemon Slices (page 226), but it uses only the zest. You can use it in the same way too, although, with this, you're more likely to use the zest and syrup separately.

MAKES ABOUT I CUP ZEST WITH SYRUP

4 lemons
1 cup sugar

1. Remove the zest from the lemons with a vegetable peeler. Cut it into needle-thin strips with a sharp knife.

2. Bring a medium saucepan of water to a boil. Add the zest, reduce the heat and simmer for 8 minutes, or until softened. Drain in a strainer and rinse the zest under cold running water. Dry on paper towels.

3. Bring the sugar and $\frac{1}{3}$ cup water to a boil in a small saucepan and stir to dissolve the sugar. Boil until the syrup reaches 230°F on a candy thermometer. Remove the pan from the heat and stir in the zest. Let stand for at least 30 minutes before using.

4. Drain the zest before using. The zest will keep, tightly covered and refrigerated in the syrup, for 4 months or more.

Lemonade Marmalade

i love this so much I've had dreams about it. The cardamom is not absolutely necessary, but it highlights the lemon flavor in the way lemon usually does other foods, and it adds a subtle and intriguing dimension. Make sure to use a large saucepan; it needs to hold at least 3 quarts, or the marmalade will boil over before it reaches 220°F. I usually divide the batch in half and add 1 tablespoon rose water to one-half. This is also very good with the addition of kaffir lime leaves.

MAKES ABOUT 2 CUPS

6 lemons
2 cups sugar
2 cardamom pods, crushed
2 tablespoons rose water, optional

1. Remove the zest from the lemons with a vegetable peeler. Cut the strips lengthwise into needle-thin strips and place in a bowl. Halve the lemons and juice them, reserving all the seeds and pulp in the juicer. Pour the lemon juice over the zest.

2. Gather all the seeds and pulp, tie them in a cheesecloth bag, and put them in a large saucepan with 2½ cups water. Let stand for at least 2 and up to 24 hours.

3. When ready to make the marmalade, add the lemon juice and zest to the saucepan, bring to a boil, and boil briskly for 20 minutes. Stir in the sugar and cardamom, reduce the heat, and simmer, stirring, until the sugar is dissolved. Return the mixture to a boil and boil until the mixture reaches 220°F on a candy thermometer.

4. Discard the bag of seeds and the cardamom pods and let the marmalade cool. Stir in the rose water, if using.

5. Pour the marmalade into jars and seal them. Store, refrigerated, for 6 months or more.

Sweet Lemon Blossom Jelly

I based this exquisitely fragrant preserve on a recipe in Rosemary Barron's wonderful and unfortunately out-of-print book, *The Flavors of Greece*, published by William Morrow. She recommends gathering the blossoms with a friend, one of you holding a bag "under a blossom-laden branch while the other gently shakes the flowers so that the petals fall into the bag." What a luxury to have enough lemon blossoms!

MAKES ABOUT 3 CUPS

2 cups sugar
1¼ cups packed (unsprayed) lemon blossoms
¼ cup fresh lemon juice
1 strip lemon zest, removed with a vegetable
   peeler, optional

1. Combine the sugar and the blossoms and let stand, uncovered, for 6 hours. Occasionally rub them together gently with your fingers.

2. Sterilize two 1-pint jars.

3. Bring ½ cup cool water and 2 tablespoons of the lemon juice just to a boil in a heavy large nonreactive saucepan over medium heat. Add the blossoms with the sugar and the zest, if using, to the saucepan. Reduce the heat to low, and cook, stirring, until the sugar is dissolved. Increase the heat to high and simmer for 20 minutes. Remove the pan from the heat, discard the zest, and let cook to room temperature.

4. Pour the mixture through a plastic strainer set over a bowl, pressing hard on the blossoms to extract as much liquid as possible. Return the syrup to the clean saucepan, add the remaining 2 tablespoons lemon juice, and bring to a boil over high heat. Boil until the syrup reaches 235°F on a candy thermometer. Let cool.

5. Fill the jars and cover tightly. The jelly will keep stored at room temperature for 2 months, or longer.

A List of Store-Bought Products for Lemon Lovers

Whole Dried Lemons

I use Swad brand from my local Indian supermarket. One package weighing one pound contains dozens (maybe hundreds) of very dark brown whole dried lemons, which look like walnuts still in their hulls and are about the same size. (And that whole bag costs less than two dollars.) If you cut a dried lemon crosswise in half you'll see that the pulp is gone, but the membranes are still intact, and the seeds are still there—looking gigantic because they don't shrink with drying as the rest of the lemon does. Their fragrance is terrific and they are wonderful added to lemonade (page 151) or tossed into stews, braises, vegetables dishes, and soups. They add a flavor quite different from that of fresh lemons, wonderful and very refreshing.

Boyajian's Pure Lemon Oil

This is a remarkably intense essence from the zest of the lemon, with no other oil added. Use it as you would fresh zest, to flavor just about anything.

You can substitute it for fresh lemon zest and/or juice in any dish and still get a fabulous true lemon flavor. It's expensive, but a little goes a very long way. I always have a bottle in my refrigerator, where it keeps indefinitely. Available in specialty foods stores and through The Bakers Catalogue (800-827-6836). I've been known to put pure lemon oil into my bath water.

Boyajian's Lemon–Black Pepper Oil

A flavored olive oil, great for savory dishes. Available in some supermarkets and specialty foods stores.

O Olive Oil Flavored with Meyer Lemons

Olive oil made from crushing organic Meyer lemons with hand-picked, family-farmed California olives with a stone press. Available in specialty foods stores.

Agrumato Lemon Extra Virgin Olive Oil

Hand-harvested olives are pressed with lemons
with a stone press in Abruzzo, Italy, to make
this oil. Available in specialty foods stores.

Lemon Powder

Chirag lemon powder is available from
www.Tavolo.com. Although this brand is made
in Guatemala, lemon powder is used in Persian
and Middle Eastern cuisine to add a tart flavor.
Made by finely grinding sun-dried lemon peel, it
looks like finely ground coffee and packs a very
intense, tart flavor. Sprinkle a tiny pinch mixed
with salt (and maybe a bit of cayenne pepper)
over cut fruit—mango would be perfect.

the practical *lemon*

Lemons Around the House

Lemons are not only magicians of flavor, they have great practical value around the house. Use them to enhance the fragrance of your home, to help with cleaning and polishing, and to decorate and add beauty.

FRAGRANCE AND BEAUTY

- For a kitchen table centerpiece, pile lemons in a footed porcelain bowl or a shallow basket. You might add fresh daisies, tiny white roses, and/or lemon leaves. You could place another bowl on your dining room table or on a shelf in your bathroom. A bowl of fresh lemons will add fragrance to the air for days and go just as far as flowers in cheering a room.

- Place a few thick strips of lemon zest on a small baking sheet in a warm oven for a few minutes to dispel lingering kitchen odors. This is especially useful after cooking fish.

- Add a handful of fresh or dried lemon zest to a fire in the fireplace for a great fragrance.

- Place small mesh bags of dried lemon zest in drawers and in closets for a very pleasing aroma.

- Eliminate odors from your humidifier by pouring 3 to 4 tablespoons of fresh lemon juice into the water.

- Keep your garbage disposal smelling fresh by grinding up lemon shells after juicing.

- To rid a plastic container of food odors, drop a lemon wedge into it, close, and let it stand until the odor disappears, up to a few days.

- Make your own potpourri: try a spicy one with strips of Oven-Dried Lemon Zest (page 15), Lemon Chips (page 22), star anise, cinnamon sticks, coriander seeds, and dried yellow rose petals. Or an herby one, with bay leaves, rosemary sprigs, Oven-Dried Lemon Zest, and Lemon Chips.

- Cut a lemon in half and scrape out all of the flesh. Trim a thin slice off the bottom of each half so they will stand steadily. Stud them with cloves, fill with potpourri, and place on decorative saucers.

- Halve lemons and scoop out all the pulp. Trim a thin slice off the bottoms of the halves so they will stand steadily. Remove the foil from tea-light candles and place them in the shells. Individual lemon cups can be placed on saucers and surrounded by small flowers or leaves. Groups of cups are also effective—cluster at least three shells together, with a small flower. Or float the

pomander balls

Pomander balls have been around for a very long time. In Shakespeare's day, it was the fashion to carry pomanders, which then were lemons or oranges from which all the pulp had been scooped out through a circular hole made at the top. After the peel had become dry, the fruit was filled with spices, so as to make a sort of scent box. Pomanders are still a treat today, to put on display in your entry hall or in a bowl on your dining room table, to scent your drawers, or to hang from a ribbon in your closet. They are attractive and have the most delightful fragrance. The orrisroot acts as a preservative.

To make pomander balls, select firm, medium-sized lemons. With the tines of a fork or a toothpick, make rows of holes in the skin from one end to the other, either as close together as possible without tearing the skin or farther apart in a pattern or design. Stick whole cloves into the holes. Roll the lemons in a small bowl of equal parts of ground cinnamon (or coriander) and orrisroot. Sprinkle the lemons with additional cinnamon and orris, until the fruit is well covered. Wrap in tissue paper or cheesecloth and let dry out for a month. If desired, tie a ribbon around each lemon so that the pomander can be hung in the closet.

shells in a pretty bowl filled with water, and light the candles.

~ Decorate your Christmas tree with Lemon Chips (page 22), tied with bright red ribbons.

~ Scented finger bowls? Not a necessity of life, but if you want to use them, fill small bowls about one-third full with warm water, add about a teaspoon of fresh lemon juice to each, and float a paper-thin lemon slice in each bowl. You might want to provide large napkins.

~ Keep your vacuum cleaner smelling clean, no matter what it's cleaning up, by putting a cotton ball soaked in lemon juice in the bag each time you change it.

PLANTS AND FLOWERS

~ To germinate lemon seeds, sow them in small flats of potting soil and keep well watered. When they're a few inches tall, transplant them to larger pots and watch them grow into lush (but probably fruitless) trees.

~ Leftover lemon shells can be used to fertilize roses or other plants that need extra acidity.

~ Use lemons instead of marbles to anchor flowers in the bottom of a vase.

Lemon slices and water will remove hard-water deposits from vases. Slice a lemon into the vase, fill it with water, and let it stand for a day or two.

Lemons which have been used in the flavoring of cabbage leaves and other such insipids may be hung on old or unused garments and will help to preserve them by keeping away moths and other predators.
—Leonardo da Vinci

FABRIC

˜ Use lemons to remove lipstick stains from fabric. If the fabric is white, soak the lipstick stain in lemon juice. If it's colored, dilute the lemon juice by half with water first.

˜ Remove ink spots from clothing by applying lemon juice while the ink is still wet, then wash the garment in cold water.

˜ To remove rust stains from washable fabric, soak the stain in lemon juice, dry the garment in the sun to bleach it out, and then rinse thoroughly.

˜ If you're traveling and splash tomato sauce on your favorite white blouse, squeeze lemon juice onto it, then wash it out.

˜ Add ½ cup fresh lemon juice during the rinse cycle of your washing machine and hang the clothes to dry in the sun for whitening.

To remove mildew stains from white fabrics, moisten with a mixture of lemon juice and salt and spread in the sun to bleach as they dry.

To whiten white canvas sneakers, add lemon juice to the final rinse cycle and let them dry in the sun.

To remove berry stains on washable white fabric, immediately rub with a lemon half, then rinse with water and let air-dry.

Bring a large pot of water and several slices of lemon to a boil. Add socks, linens, or whatever needs whitening, turn off the heat, and let sit for 30 to 60 minutes. Drain and wash as usual.

SHOES

For a high shine on your shoes or boots, rub a little bit of lemon juice into the leather after it's been polished, then buff.

For white suede shoes, brush to remove surface dirt, then rub with lemon juice and let dry in the sun.

KITCHEN AND BATHROOM

Boil lemon slices in water to add a fragrance to your kitchen. Add a cinnamon stick, cloves, coriander seeds, or a bay leaf if you feel like getting fancy.

Eliminate odors from your refrigerator by placing four or five lemon slices strategically on the shelves and in the door. Leave them for several hours, then remove.

Use the shells of juiced lemons to clean your hands after working with walnuts or berries.

Clean a stainless-steel sink by rubbing it gently with a paste of salt and lemon juice; rinse.

To get rid of a fishy smell on your hands, sprinkle powdered mustard on them and drizzle on enough lemon juice to make a paste; rub in well, then wash your hands with soap and water.

To remove odors from cutting boards, rub with a lemon half, rinse well, and dry.

To renew glass sparkle and brightness, rub with cut lemon or soak in lemon juice and water. Rinse well, and dry with a cloth that leaves no lint. (This is especially good for glass decanters and coffeepots.)

- Boil fresh lemon juice or sliced lemons in the water to remove discoloration from a tea kettle. Or clean with a cloth dipped in lemon juice and rinse in warm water.

- To remove stains from cookware such as saucepans, add a handful of kosher salt and the juice of a lemon, fill with water, and boil until the stain disappears.

- Copper pans and bowls can be scoured with kosher salt applied with a lemon half.

- If egg has dried on your patterned glass tableware, rub it off with a lemon wedge.

- To clean kitchen and bathroom drains, pour ½ cup baking soda down the drain, then add ½ cup lemon juice. You may hear some noises, but wait for 15 minutes or so before flushing with warm water.

- Rub stained enamel bathroom fixtures with a cut lemon; for stubborn stains, use a paste of fresh lemon juice and borax.

CLEANING AND POLISHING

- Lemons are environmentally friendly cleaners, great for washing windows and cutting grease.

- Gently rub a paste of 2 parts salt and 1 part lemon juice over piano keys; wipe off with a damp cloth, then buff with a dry one.

- Add a spiral of lemon zest to harsh cleaning solutions to give a lemon-fresh smell as you clean.

- Mixed with salt, lemon juice is an effective bleach and disinfectant and very safe to use, unlike chlorine bleach or ammonia, and it's pleasantly fragrant.

- When cleaning a glass-topped table, rub on a little lemon juice to make it really sparkle, then dry with newspaper.

- Remove water and other spots from the chrome on your car with lemon juice.

- Clean stained marble by sprinkling salt on the cut side of a lemon half and very gently rubbing it over the stain, then wash with just a bit of a mild soap and warm water.

- To remove stubborn tarnish on brass or copper, rub it with a piece of salted lemon rind.

- Give badly tarnished unlacquered brass or copper a soak in salt and lemon juice. The tarnish should then wipe off easily.

ETCETERA

- If you'd like to offer your guests warm towels as they do in Japanese restaurants, just moisten small washcloths or napkins with a solution of water and lemon juice, wring them out, and fold them into rectangles or roll them into cylinders. Heat in the microwave on high power until hot.

- Lemon juice can be used as invisible ink. Write with it on ordinary paper; once the lemon juice dries, the writing will be invisible until the paper is gently heated.

- When washing your dog, add lemon juice to the rinse water to minimize soap film; rinse thoroughly.

- Old lemon shells can be used to repel ants from the garden.

Lemons and Beauty

Lemons have long been used for beauty treatments, at least since the women in the court of King Louis XIV sucked on lemons to redden their lips.

HAIR

- Lemon juice is a good rinse for hair. Shampoos are alkaline and may leave a sticky residue; the acid in lemon juice dissolves the residue and makes hair more manageable as well as shinier. Combine ¼ cup fresh lemon juice with ¼ cup warm water and apply after rinsing your hair, then rinse again with water.

- Lemon juice is an effective hair lightener, especially if you dry your hair in the sun. It's not very strong, but if you paint lemon juice on your hair and sit in the sun every day for at least a week, your hair may lighten slightly.

- It is said you can change blond hair dyed green by the chlorine in swimming pools back to its original color by saturating it with ¼ cup lemon juice mixed with ¾ cup water.

- Lemon has long been used as a dandruff treatment. Squeeze the juice of 1 large lemon and apply half of it to your hair. Mix the other half with 2 cups water. Wash your hair with a mild shampoo, then rinse with water. Rinse again with the lemon juice and water mixture. Repeat every other day until the dandruff disappears.

- Adding 2 egg whites and the juice of ½ lemon to shampoo is said to give hair more body and shine.

- Lemon juice can be used as a setting lotion for hair.

- For oily hair, rinse with equal parts water and lemon juice after shampooing.

SKIN

- To keep your elbows smooth and young-looking, rub them with a lemon shell.

- Cold lemon juice compresses are said to reduce puffiness under the eyes (just don't get any of the lemon juice in your eyes).

- If you have oily skin and you're out of astringent, mix lemon juice with a little cool water, splash some on your face, and wipe off with a cotton ball. During the summer, freeze the same solution in an ice cube tray; run a cube over your face when you feel hot.

The Arabs *cultivated citrus trees as ornamental plants, especially delighting in the scent of their leaves, flowers, and fruit. They shredded the ends of twigs from orange, lemon, and other aromatic trees and used them as disposable toothbrushes.*

—Margaret Visser, *Much Depends on Dinner*

- Try a paste of sugar or salt and Lemon Oil (page 214) as an exfoliant. Some prefer the sugar over the salt scrub, as it seems to be milder and to dry out the skin less. Combine about ½ cup sugar or fine sea salt and about ¼ cup oil. Once a week, in the shower, wet your skin, then take small handfuls of the mixture and apply to your body in small circular motions. Wait for a few minutes and rinse.

- For a lemony skin freshener, mix the strained juice of 1 lemon with an equal amount of rose water. Store in the refrigerator and apply with a cotton ball.

- For a cleanser for oily skin, mix equal parts fresh lemon juice and buttermilk. Apply to your face and neck, then wipe off with cotton pads.

- For a great toner for oily skin, mix together ½ cup pure aloe gel, ½ cup cucumber juice, and the juice of ½ lemon in a jar. Store tightly covered, in the refrigerator. Shake well before using.

- For a skin-purifying lemon-honey mask, apply equal parts of fresh lemon juice and honey to your face and neck, allow to dry, and rinse with cool water.

- For a refreshing skin bracer, blend lemon juice with cold water. After washing your face, splash it on to tighten pores.

- Make a paste of salt and lemon juice and rub on rough and tough areas such as elbows, the bottoms of your feet, and knees. Wash off with cool water.

- Dab facial blemishes with lemon juice several times a day.

- To cleanse your pores, combine 1 quart boiling water, the juice of ½ lemon, and a handful of fresh mint in a large bowl. Steam your face about 12 inches above the water for 5 minutes, then splash with cool water.

HANDS

- Press your fingernails into the pithy side of a lemon rind to clean them after doing dirty chores. Lemon juice will remove stains from fingers and fingernails; simply rub them with a lemon half.

- Remove pale stains on hands with a piece of lemon peel and darker stains with lemon juice and a pumice stone.

- For softer cuticles and whiter nail tips, mix 2 cups warm water with the juice of 1 lemon and soak your fingers in it for 5 minutes; repeat weekly.

index

quick, 216–17, 220; with shallots
and garlic, 220–21
sweet, 225

Quail, 127

Radish and carrot salad, 63, 198
Raisins, golden
risotto with green apples, lemon,
and, 96
spinach with lemon and, 74
Raspberries
berry lemonade, 156
peaches and berries with lemon
and rose water, 147
Relishes, 206. *See also* Condiments
lemon, mint, and olive relish,
204
Rhubarb-strawberry lemonade,
154
Rice, adding lemon flavor to,
96
Ricotta pancakes, lemony, with
plum sauce, 172–73
Risotto
adding lemon flavor to, 96, 214
fennel and green olive, 86–87
Roden, Claudia, 216–17, 220
Root vegetables
Sunday pot roast with lemon
and, 120–21
Rosemary
lemon-rosemary butter, 183
rosemary grilled chicken, 114
rosemary salmoriglio, extra-
lemony, 181

Rose water
peaches and berries with lemon
and, 147
rose water lemonade, 152

Saffron, 96
lemon-saffron mayonnaise, 192
saffron hollandaise, 189
saffron lemonade, 153
Sage
lemon-sage butter, 183
sage-caper mayonnaise, 193
Salad(s), 49–56
adding lemon flavor to, 62–63,
198, 214, 215, 219
baby greens with broiled lemons,
51
lemony tabbouleh, 53
lentil and lemon, 56
Meyer lemon and blood orange,
with fennel, 52
Middle Eastern–style orange and
lemon, 54
oranges, onion, and olives with
preserved lemons, 219
parsley, with lemon vinaigrette,
50
potato, with lemon and parsley,
49
tomato, with lemon and basil,
55
Salad dressings, 57–60
adding lemon flavor to, 62–63,
219
lemon vinaigrette: basic, 58;
creamy, 57; parsley salad with,
50

preserved lemon vinaigrette, 59
soy and sesame oil lemon
vinaigrette, 60–61
Salmon, lemon-and-coriander-
cured, 29
Salmoriglio, rosemary, extra-
lemony, 181
Salsa(s), 206
lemon salsa verde, 197; uses for,
81, 127
Moroccan-style lemon, red
onion, and parsley salsa, 202
tomato, with lemon, 201
Salt
gremolata salt, 210
lemon, 209
lemon-coriander, 209
Sandwiches, 35
lemon-cucumber, 31
Sangria, white, 165
Sauces, 181–93. *See also*
Condiments
avgolemono, 190
butter sauces, about, 183
dipping sauce: lemon-ginger,
205; Vietnamese-style, 205
gremolata brown butter, 185
hollandaise with variations,
188–89
lemon aïoli, 191
lemon beurre blanc, 186–87
lemon black butter, 185
lemon butter with variations,
182–83
lemon-garlic butter, 184
lemon mayonnaise with
variations, 192–93
lemon-tarragon tartar sauce, 105